he Future
is Now

MARIO ALBERTI

ANTOINE CHARREYRON

THE WALL

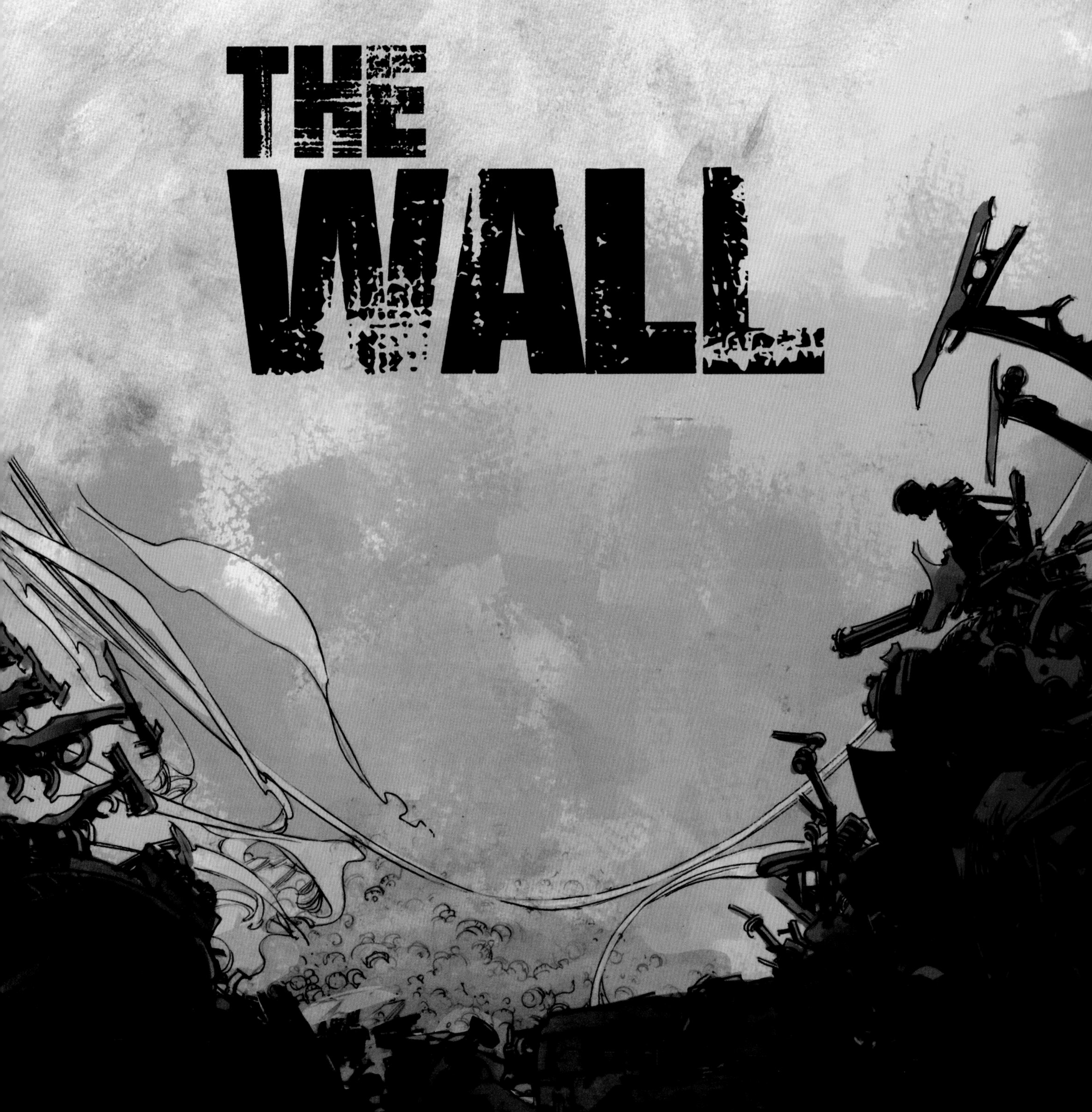

WRITTEN AND ILLUSTRATED
BY
MARIO ALBERTI

BASED ON THE STORY CREATED
BY
ANTOINE CHARREYRON

Translation by Jeremy Melloul
Localization and Editing by Mike Kennedy
Layout, Lettering, and Production Assistance by Chris Northrop

ISBN: 978-1-951719-30-2
Library of Congress Control Number: 2021913736

The Wall by Mario Alberti and Antoine Charreyron, Published 2021 by Magnetic Press, LLC.
Originally published as *Le Mur – Tome 1 : Homo Homini Lupus*, *Le Mur – Tome 2 : Homo Homini Deus*, and *Le Mur – Tome 3 : Homo Homini Spes*

Printed in China.

10 9 8 7 6 5 4 3 2 1

So here's my first attempt as a full author tackling script, drawing, and coloring. I'd like to take this opportunity to express my gratitude to Hayao Miyazaki and his work, without whom I probably would never have become an author. Especially for *Laputa, The Castle in the Sky,* which I saw many years ago convincing me that telling stories was what I would do for the rest of my life.

Thanks to Rita, Clara, and Antonio who share my love and my time in this crazy, crazy, crazy job.

Thank you to all the friends and colleagues who have shown their support for me with advice and kind words.

A special thank you to Marina Sanfelice for having beautifully written this album, to Olivier Jalabert for trusting me, and to Antoine Charreyron's invaluable help. We make an awesome team!

And for all those who build bridges and destroy walls.

Mario

Thanks to Audrey, Noam and Eliam, who travel the world with me.

Thanks to Samantha Vincent, Tarik Hamdine, Yoan Parent, François Baranger, Corentin Maignien dit Lejam, Philippe Guyenne, JD Morvan, and Bengal for their advice and investment at the start of the project.

Thanks to Olivier Jalabert, the Glénat team, and the exceptional Mario Alberti, who allowed me to make this childhood dream come true.

Antoine

INTRODUCTION

Fall 2011. I'm in Los Angeles when Nicolas Sarkozy, in conflict with Italy, alludes to the creation of a wall that would surround Europe to prevent the waves of refugees. Alone in my apartment, I find it shocking, especially since here the subject of a wall with Mexico is already very sensitive.

I spent the following days writing the first draft of *The Wall*, a film that would follow the journey of two kids lost in a world in distress. Their only hope: to cross the wall in order to find medicine, food and surely a better life. The groundwork for the project has been laid and I'm talking to Samantha Vincent, executive producer of *Fast and Furious* and the sister of Vin Diesel. She loves the project, so we move forward with development, but the budget necessary to create such a universe stops the process. It's too expensive... too big for me.

The Wall then goes into the "pending projects" box like so many others. But this story stuck with me as the fashion for comic book adaptations took off in the motion picture industry. CAA, the agency that represents me in the United States, even has a room with hundreds of comics just waiting for one thing: to be adapted onto the big or small screen.

It's a revelation. If I can't make a film out of it, *The Wall* will become a comic book, and I know who to call for that... While directing my film *The Prodigies*, I had met a great editor, Olivier Jalabert, a kind of Al Pacino of the publishing. The kind you high-five and feel like things are going to be done and that it'll be good!

We talk about the project, he loves it and then… nothing. *The Wall* is one of the projects that I've carried the longest within me, but in reality, during all this time, Olivier was looking for the ideal artist. The one who would sublimate this universe with his humanity, his sensitivity, and his talent: Mario Alberti.

This genius for detail immediately understands my desires, and the collaboration accelerates. Working with Mario is like sitting in a Formula 1 car next to Lewis Hamilton - like wind in my hair, even though I don't have much hair.

In the end, *The Wall* becomes *Le Mur* and, ironically, this story that started out in a Franco-Italian conflict about migrants is now produced by an Italian and a Frenchman… Thank you Nicolas Sarkozy, thanks to you, I have realized one of my dreams!

Antoine Charreyron

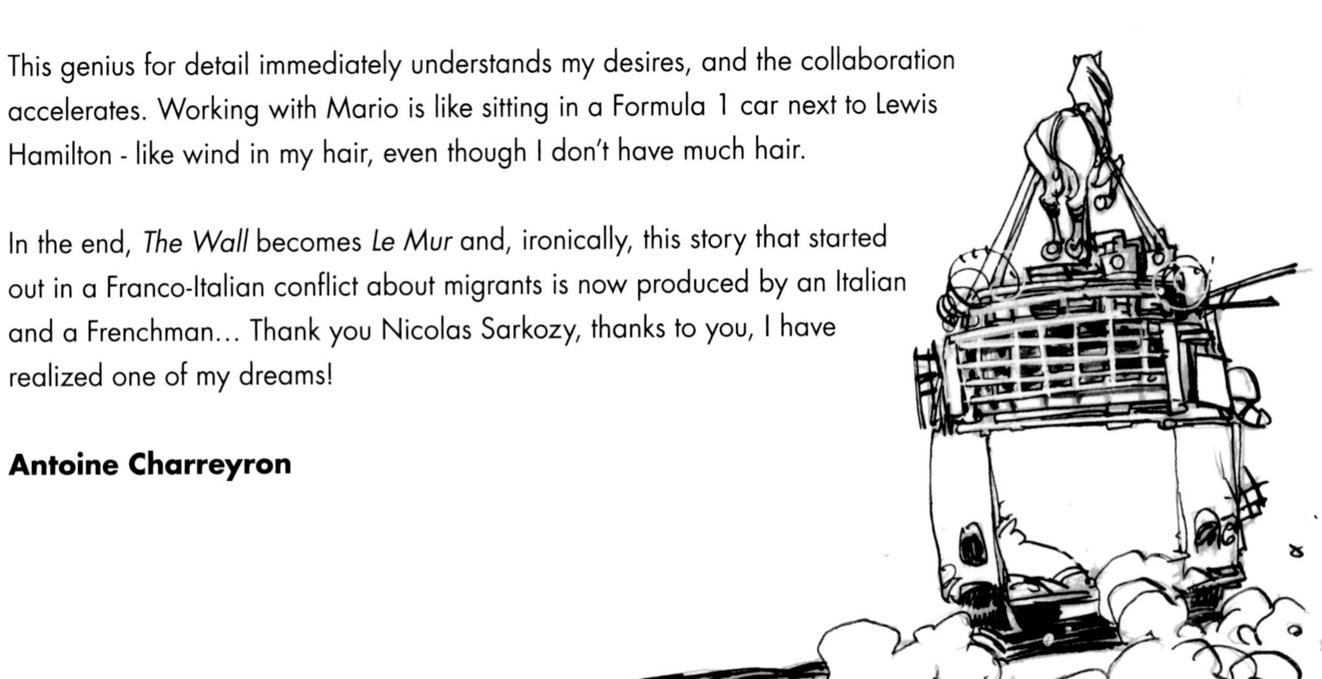

CHAPTER 1 – HOMO HOMINI LUPUS

HURRY UP, IT'LL BE NIGHT SOON!
SOLAL!
WAIT!
EVA!
AH!
PUT THAT DUMB THING AWAY AND WATCH WHERE YOU'RE WALKING. WE HAVE TO KEEP A LOW PROFILE...
IT'S NOT A DUMB THING...
PUT IT AWAY!
IT'S NOT DUMB...
...AND YOU'RE THE ONE BEING LOUD.
CLANG
SOLAL...

...LOOK!
CLANG
SHIT!

MISTER!
SHIT!

DON'T COME ANY CLOSER!

I'M ARMED!
WAIT!

I HAVE PARTS.
I COULD FIX YOUR ENGINE.

AND WHY WOULDN'T I JUST FILL YOU WITH LEAD AND TAKE YOUR BAG, KID?

BECAUSE... WE STILL BELIEVE THERE'S A LITTLE BIT OF GOOD LEFT IN THE WORLD...?

VRRR
WHAT?

YOU'VE NEVER SEEN A HORSE?
NOT REALLY... NOT LIKE THAT...
VRRR
WHERE'S IT FROM?

FROM THE PAST.
WHEN WE COULD STILL PRETEND TO BE HAPPY.

I STILL CAN! WITH MOM'S CONSOLE!

GOOD FOR YOU, GIRL. WHERE ARE YOU TWO HEADED?

WE WANT TO CROSS THE WALL. TO GET INTO EDEN.

GET OUT!

HEY!
WE'VE ALREADY BEEN THROUGH THIS! REMEMBER?

I WON'T GO BACK!

PUT THE GUN DOWN, OLD MAN...

GET AWAY!

SHIT!
GRRGR

NO!
EVA! GET IN THE VAN!

4

GRAAAR

SLAM

THAT GUY WAS REALLY FREAKING OUT...
FORGET ABOUT HIM.
WE HAVE TO HURRY. NOW THAT WE HAVE THIS VAN, WE CAN TRADE IT FOR PASSAGE.
...REALLY FREAKING...
EVA!
HAN HAN
HERE...
FT!
...TAKE THIS.
WE'LL BE THERE SOON.
THEY'LL HAVE ALL THE MEDICINE AND ANYTHING ELSE WE MIGHT NEED.
AND BETTER FOOD TO EAT, TOO...
STOP IT! THAT DOG WASN'T THAT BAD...

YOU'RE GONNA HAVE TO TAKE THE WHEEL...
EMPTY...
CLAK

SOLAL!

GET BACK OR I'LL BLOW YOUR HEAD OFF!

FIRST PERSON TO COME ANY CLOSER GETS SHOT!

YOU GOT A NICE GUN AND A NICE RIDE THERE, BOY...
...I BET SOME PEOPLE'D BE WILLING TO KILL FOR THAT.

I'M NOT HERE TO BET. I'M HERE TO MAKE A TRADE.

THE VAN FOR PASSAGE OVER THE WALL...

...THE HORSE COMES WITH IT.

YOU SELLING STOLEN GOODS, KID?

THAT'S B.A.S.T.A.R.D.'S LOGO, RIGHT THERE.

8

YOU'D BE BETTER OFF FOLLOWING THE OLD PIPELINE TO FIND HIM AND GIVE HIM BACK HIS VAN.

HE MIGHT EVEN LISTEN TO YOU BEFORE KILLING YOU AND YOUR LADY.

I'M HIS SISTER!

SHUT UP, EVA.

B.A.S.T.A.R.D. IS THE ONLY ONE WHO KNOWS HOW TO CROSS OVER.
I'LL GO WITH YOU.

NO! DON'T LISTEN TO HER!

I'LL GIVE YOU ALL MY AMMO IF YOU TAKE ME AWAY FROM HERE!

FORGET THE WALL! FORGET EDEN!
THERE'S ONLY DEATH OVER THERE!

BANG

AND THAT'S WHAT HAPPENS WHEN YOU TRY TO STEAL FROM B.A.S.T.A.R.D.

NOMEN OMEN.

SHUT YOUR TRAP.

EVERYBODY LISTEN UP! THAT VAN BELONGS TO ME!
THAT RIFLE BELONGS TO ME!
HIS AMMO BELONGS TO ME!

THIS CORPSE BELONGS TO ME!

SO BRING ME THE DESERTER WHO STOLE MY VAN OR I'LL BURN EVERYTHING DOWN...

HE'S NOT HERE...

WHO THE HELL ARE YOU?

I FIXED THE VAN AND DROVE IT HERE... THE OLD MAN IS DEAD.
WE WANT TO GET OVER THE WALL!
A MECHANIC, HUH? I'LL GIVE YOU A CHANCE TO PROVE YOUR USEFULNESS. OTHERWISE...
LEAVE MY BROTHER ALONE!
WHAT DO WE HAVE HERE? A TIGRESS? OR A LITTLE KITTEN?
PLEASE, B.A.S.T.A.R.D.. THE GIRL DOESN'T KNOW WHAT SHE'S SAYING...
...THERE'S NO NEED TO...
TAKE TWENTY MEN AND TWENTY WOMEN!
SHOW ME YOU CAN FIX YOUR BROTHER'S NOSE, KITTY CAT.
I'LL GIVE YOU ONE CHANCE.

"KILL ANYONE WHO RESISTS."
CAN YOU IMAGINE?
ATLANTROPA
DANGER
WATER... WATER AS FAR AS YOU COULD SEE.
I WAS YOUNG. I BARELY REMEMBER WHEN THEY ALL DRIED UP.
THEY USED TO CALL IT THE MEDITERRANEAN.
THE WALL... EDEN... WHAT DO YOU KNOW ABOUT IT, SOLAL?
I KNOW THAT EVA WILL DIE WITHOUT HER MEDICINE AND THAT IT'S BEEN MONTHS SINCE WE'VE FOUND ANY MORE OUT HERE...
...WHAT ELSE WOULD I NEED TO KNOW?
THAT MIGRANTS AREN'T WELCOME IN THESE PARTS...
...YOU'LL HAVE TO FIGHT.

WELL THEN, WE'LL FIGHT.
AND WE'LL GET THROUGH IT.

WHERE'S THE NEW GIRL?
?
YOU'RE THE DOCTOR? I FIXED SOLAL'S NOSE!
APPARENTLY YOU DIDN'T DO A VERY GOOD JOB. I'M THE BUTCHER.
WHERE ARE YOU TAKING HER?!
NO! STOP! SOLAL!
LEAVE HER ALONE!
HEY!
SOLAL!
KOF! KOF!

LET GO OF ME!
KOF KOF
EVA! TAKE YOUR MEDICINE!
PFF
HN... HN...
EVA!
TAKE IT EASY, DUDE.
WHAK
PFT

KARL?

CHANDRA...?

THAT KID...
IS HE...?
NO,
KARL.

I DID
EVERYTHING
I COULD TO
PROTECT OUR
SON, BUT...
...I'M SORRY.

YOUR SISTER FELL ASLEEP.

HOW DID HE GO?
A FEVER. A MONTH AGO.

I'M AT MY LIMIT, KARL.

I CAN'T KEEP DOING THIS ALONE. I NEED YOU TO TAKE CARE OF ME.

YOU CAN COUNT ON ME.

THE "BAIT"! NO WEAPONS, NO ARMOR. JUST PURE SPEED!
THE NEW ONES ARE YOURS!
WATCH THEM CLOSELY!
GET FRIENDLY!
HEY! I COULD USE A HAND HERE!
SOLAL!
YOU'RE HERE...
MECHANIC, REMEMBER?
?
MARCELO!
18

WHAT'S SHE DOING HERE WITH THE BAIT PILOTS?!
HUH? WHY WOULD I KNOW? ASK B.A.S.T.A.R.D.!

YOU NOW ME, KARL. MY THING IS ROCKETS AND PISTONS...
...NOT PILOTS!

FINALLY! SOMEONE WHO CAN APPRECIATE MARCELO'S WORK!

THAT MUCH IS OBVIOUS! THIS MACHINE MIGHT JUST BE A HUNK OF METAL, BUT I BET IT RUNS LIKE A MISSILE!

TAKE A LOOK AT THIS ENGINE!

I ALSO KNOW HOW HARD IT IS TO FIND REPLACEMENT PARTS!

HONESTLY... I PREFER THESE LITTLE RACERS TO THOSE LARGE, OVER-GEARED MACHINES!

AH!

YOU BETTER BRING HER BACK TO ME IN ONE PIECE, PILOT!

I'LL DO MY BEST...

THE STEERING ON THE BAITS ARE BROKEN... ONCE THEY START THEY JUST GO STRAIGHT AHEAD...
I KNOW. I'VE ALREADY DRIVEN ONE.
AND THEN WHAT? WHY ARE YOU LETTING IT HAPPEN?
WE LIVE IN A SHIT WORLD, KID.
BUT I CAN'T LET THEM PUT CHANDRA BEHIND THE WHEEL OF ONE OF THOSE KAMIKAZE MACHINES.
AND I CAN'T LET EVA DIE WITHOUT DOING ANYTHING....
...OR PRETEND LIKE EVERYTHING'S GOING TO BE ALRIGHT.
I HAVE TO GET OVER THE WALL.
I'LL TAKE CARE OF THE STEERING ON CHANDRA'S BAIT...
...I HAVE A PLAN...

"...MORE OR LESS..."
VROOM
VROOM
HE'S NOT ALLOWED TO TAKE MY SPOT! UNTIE ME.
SORRY, CHANDRA. YOU'RE STUCK HERE WITH ME.
JUST UNTIL THEY GET BACK!
YOU'LL BE STUCK HERE ALONE! HE WON'T COME BACK!
WE STILL HAVE TIME TO STOP HIM!
I'M BEGGING YOU...!
VROOM VROOM
VROOM

DESTINY MADE US BASTARDS!
WE WHO WERE BORN ON THE WRONG SIDE OF THE WALL!
YOU LIKE STORIES, CHANDRA? I LOVED THE ONES MY MOM SAVED FOR US ON HERE...
"SOLAL HATES THEM BECAUSE... WELL, HE'S A BOY, Y'KNOW?"
"BUT FOR ME, I... I CAN STILL HEAR HER VOICE..."
"...AND I'M SURE SOLAL CAN, TOO."
HE PROMISED HER THAT HE'D NEVER ABANDON ME...
"DO YOU WANT ME TO TELL YOU A STORY, CHANDRA?"
B.A.S.T.A.R.D. IS OUR NAME!
NOMEN OMEN!
NOMEN OMEN!
DEAD RABBIT
FUCK DESTINY.
ROO

WOOSHH
THE DRONE!

BAIT DRIVERS!
MOVE UP!

ROCKETS iN POSITiON!
VROOMM
MAKE SURE THEY CONCENTRATE ON THE BAiT!

HE'S COMING! CERBERUS!
PREPARE TO FIRE!
VROOO
27

ZAP
BRAAM
ROO
FIRE!

WHAT'D THAT IDIOT KID DO?!
WHO WAS DRIVING THAT DAMN BAIT?
THE NEW MECHANIC.

BANG
WATCH OUT! CERBERUS IS STILL ACTIVE!
FALL BACK!
RETREAT!

"HE'S GOING BACK INTO THE WALL!"
FIND ME KARL.
"OR WHAT'S LEFT OF HIS BODY."
32

WE HAVE AN INTRUDER.
START SEARCHING. WE HAVE TO FIND THEM.
STLAK!
34

...AND KUNTI SAID: "DRAUPADI WILL HAVE FIVE HUSBANDS!"
THEY'RE BACK.
VRRR
YOU CAN UNTIE ME NOW.

KARL!
WHY WAS THAT DAMN KID IN ONE OF THE BAITS? YOU HAD ORDERS!

WE...
≡KOF≡
...WE MADE A DEAL...

...HE SAVES HIS SISTER... ≡KOF≡
...I SAVE MY WIFE...

FUCK OFF, KARL. RULES ARE RULES.

35

I GIVE THEM, YOU FOLLOW THEM!

GO GET ME THAT KID'S SISTER.

YOU HAVE SIX HOURS TO GET US IN BEFORE WE MAKE ANOTHER ATTEMPT.

WHAT?! THAT'S IMPOSSIBLE! I'VE GOT ROBOTS ON MY HEELS! I...

THEN DON'T GET CAUGHT. HERE -- TALK TO SOMEONE WHO'LL BE DRIVING A BAIT IN OUR NEXT CHARGE...

ANYTHING TO SAY, TIGRESS?

DESTROY THE SOURCE.

RADIO SIGNAL DETECTED.

SHIT!

SOLAL!

CRASH
AND SHIT!
AAAAH
BIP
SCAN COMPLETE. ACCESS GRANTED.

38

FUCK!

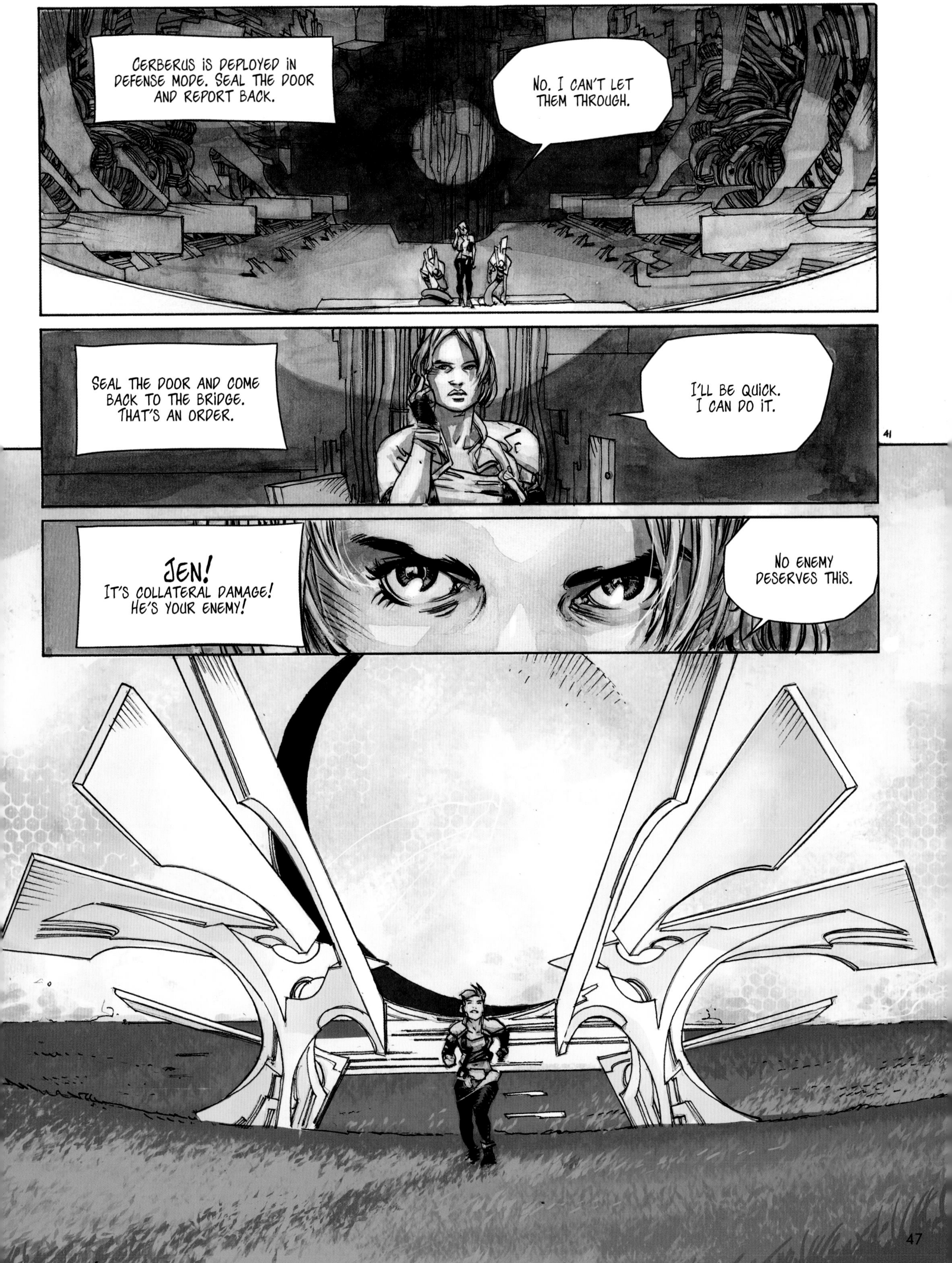

Cerberus is deployed in defense mode. Seal the door and report back.
No. I can't let them through.

Seal the door and come back to the bridge. That's an order.
I'll be quick. I can do it.

41

Jen! It's collateral damage! He's your enemy!

No enemy deserves this.

YOU'RE A BAD PERSON.
GOOD OR BAD... THOSE WORDS MEAN NOTHING HERE, TIGRESS.
BECAUSE YOU DON'T LIKE ANYONE.
RAAAHHHH!
CRASH

43

UH... HELLO?
SHIT!
HSSS
NO!
THUD
THE PILLS!
45

WAIT!

THE MEDICINE!

THERE'S NO TIME!

WHAT WAS THAT THING?!

SPRKAH
SHIT!
URRGH
BHAM
IS THAT ONE OF YOUR DRONES?
NO, IT'S NOT ONE OF MINE!
YOU IDIOT! YOU STILL DON'T UNDERSTAND?
WE'RE NOT TRYING TO STOP YOU FROM GETTING IN HERE...

"...WE'RE TRYING TO STOP THEM FROM GETTING OUT!"

CHAPTER 2 – HOMO HOMINI DEUS

"EUROPE."

"AFRICA."

"EXPIRATION, INSPIRATION. EXPANSION, CONTRACTION. FULL AND EMPTY..."

It's the storm and the ark, Cliff. But with a lot less water.
Then your name is rather apt, Noah.
You should let your beard grow... like all good patriarchs. But I'm sure your marketing team told you that a clean shaven face would elicit more tickets to Eden.
Exactly.
People hate difficult questions.
But they love easy answers.
Boss?
The Captain wishes to inform you that we're approaching Eden.

LADIES AND GENTLEMEN, PLEASE HEAD TOWARDS THE ELEVATORS.
LAST CALL.
SIR, WE HAVE A PROBLEM.

PLEASE!
HELP US!

FORM A PERIMETER!!!

WHAT'S GOING ON?
LAURA! TAKE CARE OF OUR GUESTS!
WE'LL TAKE CARE OF THIS.
LIFT 1
LIFT 2
LIFT 3

BUT... THERE ARE KIDS IN THE WATER...
LIFT 1

WE'RE NOT A REFUGEE CAMP.
PROTECT OUR GUESTS FROM THOSE UNDESIRABLES.

DIRTY PARASITES.
BUT, BOSS...

CAN I BORROW THIS FROM YOU, YOUNG MAN?
ALRIGHT, EVERYBODY! DON'T PAY ANY ATTENTION TO THAT! WE'VE STILL GOT PLENTY TO DRINK IN EDEN!
LIFT 1
LIFT 2

KEEP CALM AND CONTINUE WITH THE WELCOME PROCESS.
COUNTERMEASURES ARE ALREADY IN PLACE.
LIFT 1

BABA!

LET GO OF MY SISTER!
HEY!

NO!
HELP!
GIVE ME THAT CHILD!
STOP!

STAY WITH ME!

PLEASE!
KEEP CALM AND HEAD FOR YOUR ASSIGNED ELEVATOR!

NOAH!
WAIT!

DON'T PUSH!
HEY!
FORM A LINE!

GET BACK!
ARGH!
STAY NEAR ME!
HOLD YOUR BREATH!

OKAY, EVERYBODY!
LET'S TAKE THE GLOVES OFF!
SWITCH TO LIVE AMMO!

HELP! PLEASE! I BEG YOU!
WE'RE ALMOST THERE!

BANG

BRRT BRRT

NOAH!
NO!
BRRT

DEPLOY CERBERUS.

NOAH.

BRRR

NO...
NOO

I WANT TO BRING THAT MONSTER TO ITS KNEES.
I WANT YOU TO BUILD THE BIGGEST ROCKET YOU CAN MANAGE, MARCELO.
I WANT YOU TO USE EVERYTHING WE'VE GOT. IT'S OUR ONLY CHANCE.
THE DRONE CAME BACK IN FLAMES. CERBERUS IS RIGHT HERE...
IT'S HIGH TIME FOR THE B.A.S.T.A.R.D.S TO BRING DOWN THAT WALL AND EVERYTHING IT PROTECTS.

SNIF
WHAT?!
I UNDERSTAND, BOSS. EVERYONE LIKES BIG BOMBS... BUT...
WHAT?!
WE HAVE A GUY INSIDE. FOR THE FIRST TIME. YOU GAVE HIM SIX HOURS...
...MAYBE HE'S STILL ALIVE?
THAT "GUY" IS JUST A KID. HE'S PROBABLY DEAD MEAT BY NOW.
SOLAL ISN'T DEAD.
HE'S GOING TO COME BACK WITH MY MEDICATION.
HE PROMISED.

MOVE!
THUD
DON'T MAKE ANY NOISE. STAY HIDDEN.
DO AS I SAY.
NO MATTER WHAT HAPPENS, I CAN'T LET THEM GET YOU.
WHY?
I GOT THIS FAR. I'M NOT LEAVING WITHOUT THAT MEDICINE.
I COULD DISTRACT THEM. YOU GO FIND THE MEDICINE AND THEN WE GET OUT OF HERE.
SOUND GOOD?
YOU'RE CRAZY.
I DON'T HAVE A CHOICE: MY SISTER WILL BE PART OF THE NEXT ATTACK... AFTER THAT, NOTHING ELSE WILL MATTER.
THEY'RE GONNA ATTACK? AGAIN?!
THEY'LL NEVER GIVE UP. NO MATTER HOW MANY OF THEM YOU KILL.
WE HAVE TO MOVE! NOW!
OH, GOD!

I COULD USE YOUR GUN...

SHIT!

WE LEFT LAURA... SHE WAS YOUR ASSISTANT FOR MORE THAN... TEN YEARS?
NOT SOME RANDOM PERSON YOU COULD JUST FORGET...

HONESTLY, CLIFF: SHE KNEW WHAT WAS GOING TO HAPPEN.
WE ALL KNEW.

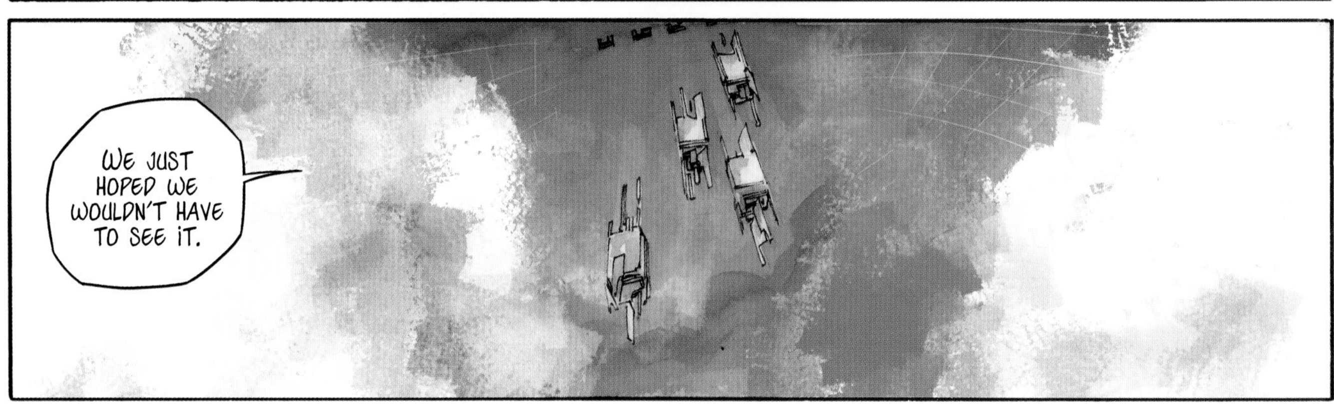
WE JUST HOPED WE WOULDN'T HAVE TO SEE IT.

"WE'LL FORGET."
DAD!
JANOS!
LAURA TOOK MY BALL!
I WANT MY CRYSTAL BALL BACK!
DON'T WORRY ABOUT IT, KIDDO.
WE'LL FIND YOU PLENTY OF OTHER TOYS, HERE.
CHAMPAGNE?
EDEN

In mom's stories, men like you always end up getting killed by their own people...

...Is that why you killed Karl?

He wouldn't understand... I made them.

You're just mean.
And stupid.

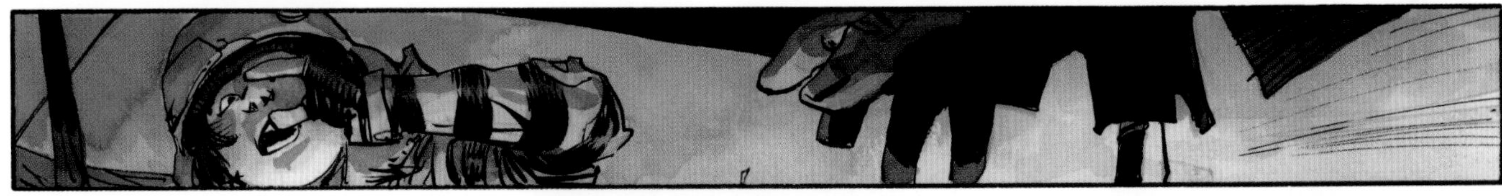

"Mean"? Do you know what "mean" is, Tigress? Look at that monster over there.

It's just a machine. Machines aren't good or bad.

You're right: neither good nor bad. No choice. Just one goal...
...Same as me.

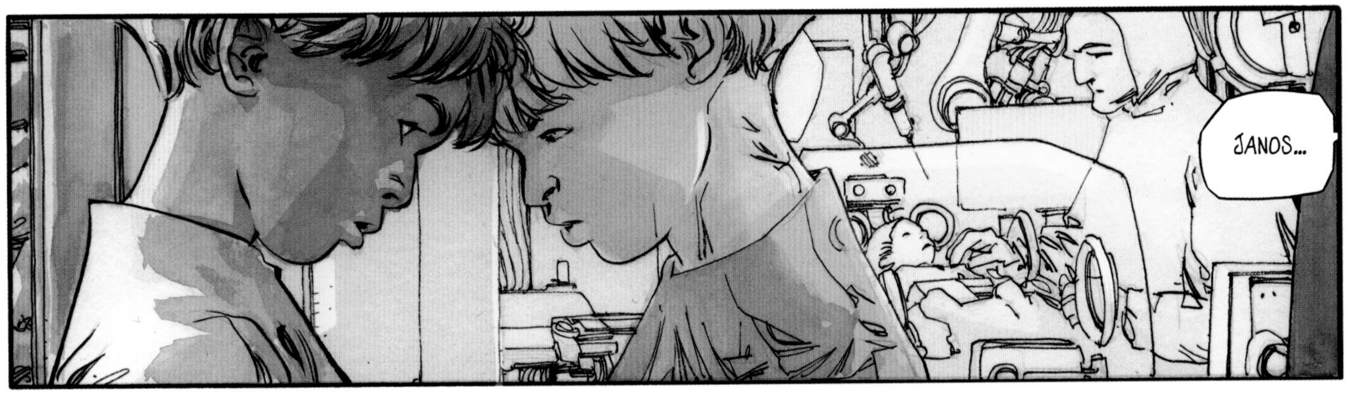
JANOS...

...SHE'LL BE ALRIGHT.

EVERYTHING WILL GO BACK TO THE WAY IT WAS.
HELL IN ED3N
NOAH DICKHEAD
WE PAID FOR

"NO MATTER WHAT'S WRONG WITH THESE PEOPLE..."
"...YOUR FATHER WILL NEVER LET YOUR SISTER OR HIS CREATION FAIL."

"HE'S A MAGICIAN. HE ALWAYS HAS A CARD UP HIS SLEEVE."

WHAT...?

No!
No!

Stay away from me!!

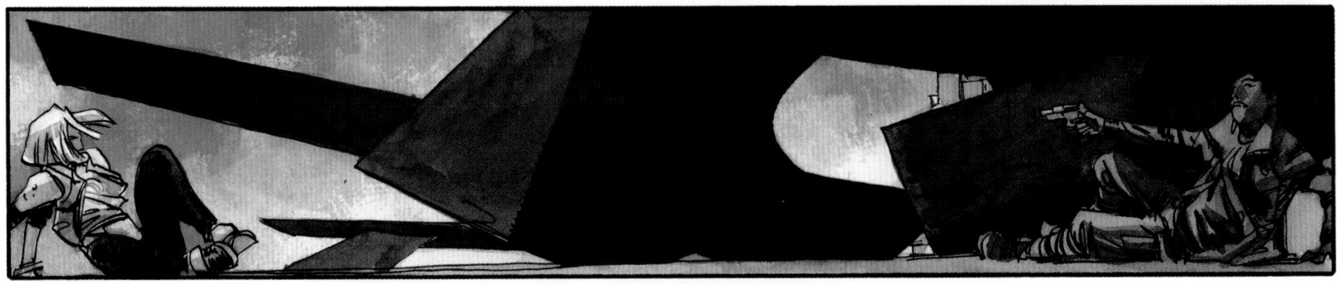

What was that?
What were you doing to me?

THAT THING ON YOUR BODY...
...iT'S THE SAME AS THEiRS!
WHAT iS iT?
IT'S AN ENERGY ORB. IT'S KEEPiNG ME ALiVE.
IT FEEDS OFF EVERYTHiNG iT TOUCHES.
INCLUDiNG THE HEAT FROM YOUR BODY...

IT WAS BEGiNNiNG TO ABSORB YOUR ENERGY.
I WAS WEAKENED. YOU WERE TOO CLOSE.

YOU MUST NEVER GET CLOSE TO ME.

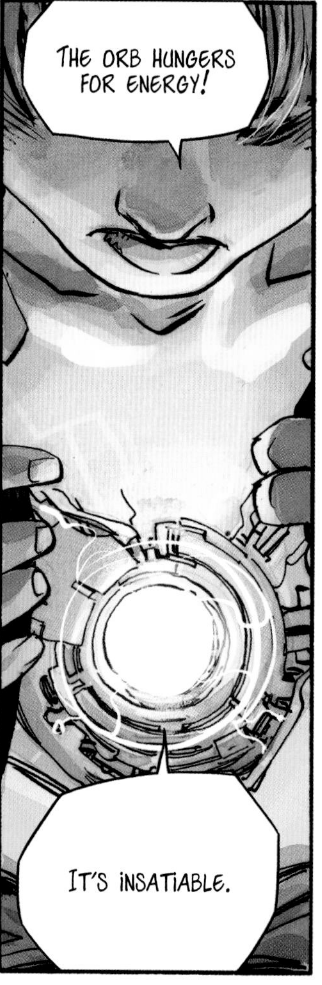

THE ORB HUNGERS FOR ENERGY!
IT'S iNSATiABLE.

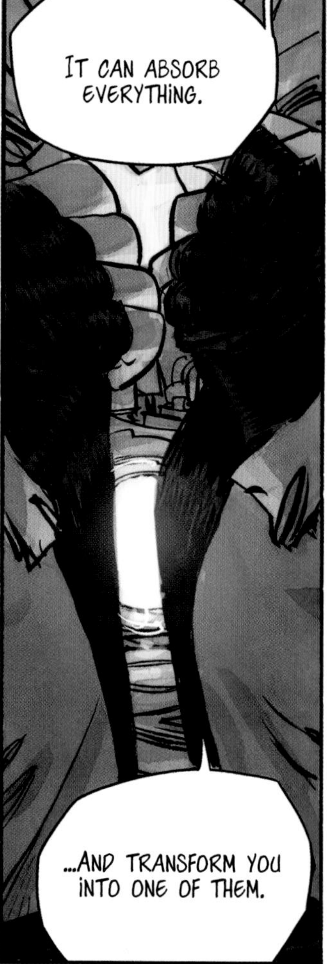

IT CAN ABSORB EVERYTHiNG.
...AND TRANSFORM YOU iNTO ONE OF THEM.

JANOS! WHAT ARE YOU DOING HERE?

I'M LOOKING AT THE SKY. IT'S BEAUTIFUL, ISN'T IT?
DAD DOESN'T WANT ANYONE ON THE ROOF.
IT'S DANGEROUS.

NO. IT'S REALLY NOT.

HE JUST DOESN'T WANT ANYONE TO SEE WHAT HE INFLICTED UPON THE WORLD.
HE WANTS US TO STAY IN HIS BOX FOREVER.

AS POORLY PROTECTED AS SCHRODINGER'S CATS!

BANG
DON' LET THOSE MONKEYS SCARE YOU.
"THEY CAN'T CLIMB."

DO YOU SMELL THAT, TIGRESS?
THE SCENT OF FEAR?

YOU PET YOUR GUN LIKE IT'S AN ANIMAL...

WHAT IS THAT? A CONSOLE?

WHERE'D YOU FIND THAT CONSOLE?!

LEAVE ME ALONE!
CRAASH

SHIT.

TELL ME...
... WHAT HAPPENED?
WHY DO YOU CARE?
YOU WERE ONLY INTERESTED IN WHAT WE HAVE.

BUT WE HAVE NOTHING LEFT. JUST THEM. THE UNDEAD. AND A BEAUTIFUL ARTIFICIAL SUN.

WHY NOT TURN OFF THE SUN?

WOULDN'T THEY ALL DIE IF YOU DID?
WOULD YOU DO THAT TO YOUR FAMILY?

"EVEN IF THEY WERE MONSTERS?"

DON'T GET TOO CLOSE.
JUST GO AROUND THE LAMP...

AND YOU'RE BACK. GOOD JOB, SIS!

OOF! IT'S HOT UNDER THAT HELMET.
YOU'LL GET USED TO IT. PUT IT BACK ON.
JUST REMEMBER: WE'LL FLY IN THE DRONES TOGETHER SOON!

HEY!
MOM!
ARE THE TWO OF YOU TRYING TO KILL ME?

YOU'RE READY. YOUR DAD IS WAITING FOR YOU IN THE AUDITORIUM.

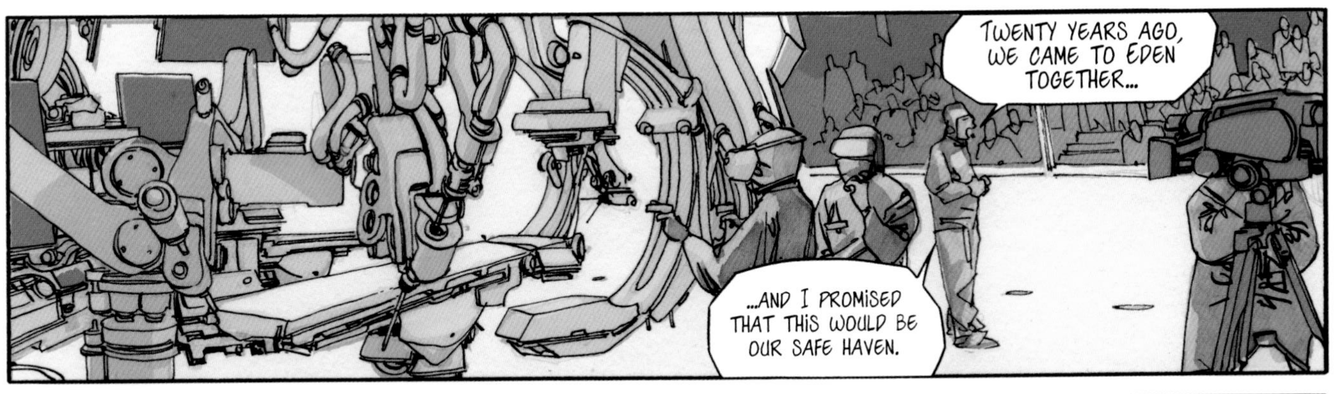
TWENTY YEARS AGO, WE CAME TO EDEN TOGETHER...
...AND I PROMISED THAT THIS WOULD BE OUR SAFE HAVEN.

WE'VE PRESERVED OUR WAY OF LIFE HERE.
TECHNOLOGY PROTECTS US BY DEFENDING THE WALL. THAT SAME TECHNOLOGY WILL SAVE OUR LIVES...

DESIGNED TO TAKE EVERYTHING A HUMAN NEEDS FROM THE ENVIRONMENT, THE ORB WILL ADAPT TO YOUR ANATOMY LIKE A GLOVE.
OR LIKE A STRAW IN YOUR FAVORITE COCKTAIL, BUT WITHOUT EVEN NEEDING TO THINK ABOUT DRINKING.
THE ORB FUNCTIONS LIKE A LUNG -- IT'S AUTOMATIC. AND JUST LIKE YOUR NOSE, YOU'LL QUICKLY FORGET THAT YOU HAVE ONE IN YOUR CHEST!

YOU LIKE DAD'S JOKES? BECAUSE I DON'T...
ARE YOU SCARED, JANOS?
WITHOUT FURTHER ADO, LET ME INTRODUCE YOU TO THE FIRST SPECIMEN OF NEW HUMANS...

DON'T WORRY, SIS. I WON'T ABANDON YOU.
...MY SON AND DAUGHTER, JANOS AND JEN!

"EVEN BEREFT OF THEIR HUMANITY, WOULD YOU KILL THE ONES YOU LOVE?"
SAMPLE REFUSED.
"EVEN IF THEY HAD LOST THEIR SOULS?"
I... I DON'T KNOW.
I DO. YOU WOULDN'T DO IT.
HERE. I FOUND SOME MEDICINE...
...I'LL LEAVE IT HERE.
NOW STAY AWAY FROM ME.
YOUR PLACE IS OUTSIDE. MINE IS ON THE DRONE... BEFORE YOUR STUPID FRIENDS DECIDE TO ATTACK US AGAIN...
"...ONLY TO DIE ON THE BATTLEFIELD."
WHY TAKE CARE OF THE GIRL, B.A.S.T.A.R.D.?
SHE RAN AWAY, SO WHAT?

I'LL MAKE YOU EAT YOUR OWN BRAIN IF WE DON'T FIND HER.
THAT'S WHAT.

SHE'LL COME BACK...

NO, SHE WON'T.

SHE WENT TO GO LOOK FOR HER BROTHER...

...THAT'S WHAT YOUNG TIGERS DO.

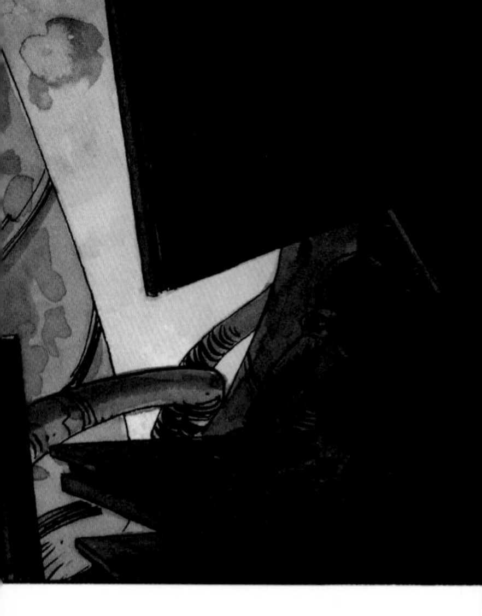

"THE SUN IS LOW."

"THEY'RE STARTING TO SENSE MY ORB."
"THEY KNOW WE'RE CLOSE."

"BUT THEY CAN BARELY MOVE."
WE'RE GOING TO HAVE TO GET PAST THEM.
ANY ADVICE?

NO MATTER WHAT HAPPENS...
...DON'T LET THEM TOUCH YOU.

"WILL THEY NEVER LEARN?"
IS THE DRONE READY?
JUST AWAITING ORDERS, SIR.
SEND IT INTO EDEN. I WANT JEN HERE AND THE INTRUDER TAKEN PRISONER.
THAT'S NO SIMPLE INTRUDER.
ACTIVATE CERBERUS.
THE KID'S D.N.A. IS IN THE DATABASE! JEN SAW IT. YOU CAN'T JUST GET RID OF HIM LIKE THAT. JUST LIKE YOU CAN'T GET RID OF EVERYONE OUTSIDE.
JEN WILL NEVER LET CERBERUS ATTACK WITHOUT HER.
JEN SHOULD NEVER HAVE GONE INTO EDEN FOR A SINGLE MISERABLE LIFE.
SHE'S RESPONSIBLE FOR THE BLOOD THAT WILL FLOW TODAY.
"IT'S TIME FOR EVERYONE TO LEARN THAT LESSON."

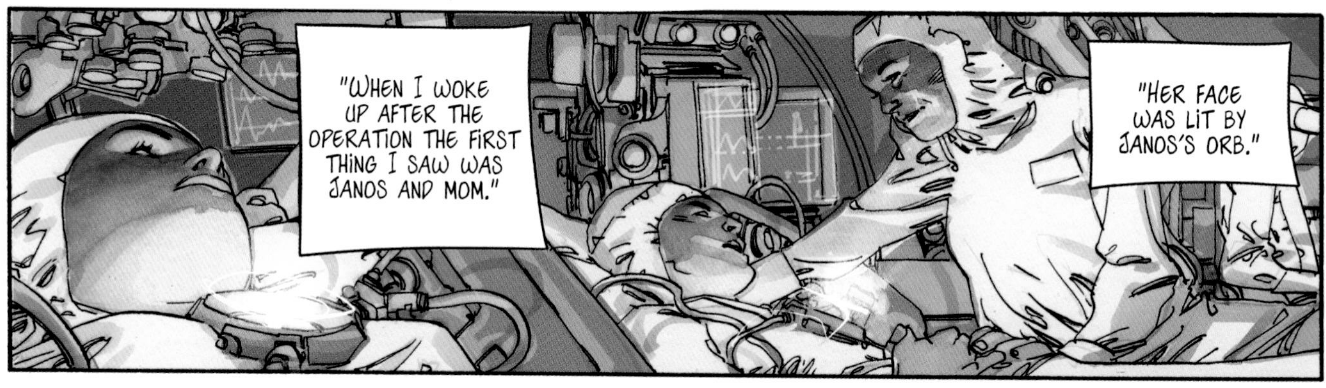
"WHEN I WOKE UP AFTER THE OPERATION THE FIRST THING I SAW WAS JANOS AND MOM."
"HER FACE WAS LIT BY JANOS'S ORB."

"AND THEN DAD. HE WAS TOUCHING MY FEET."
CAN YOU FEEL THAT?
"I FELT IT."
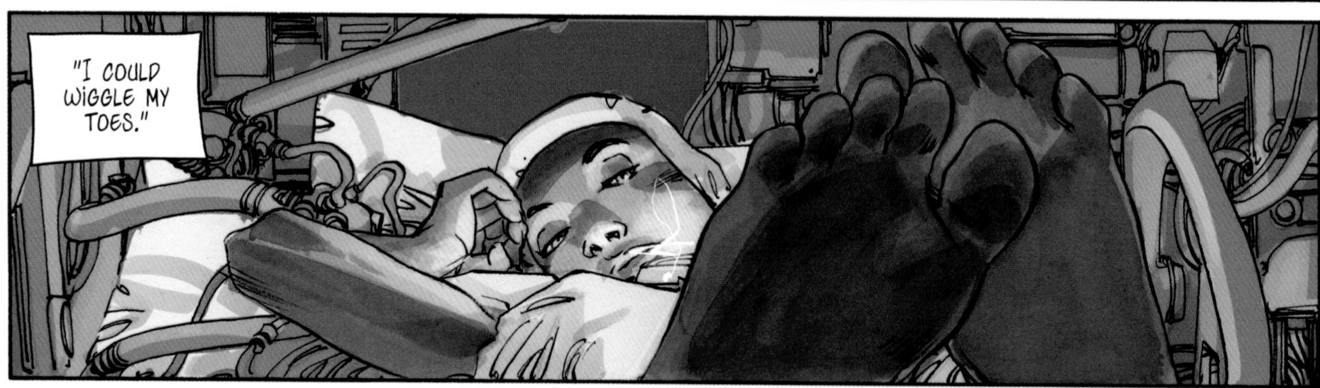
"I COULD WIGGLE MY TOES."

"I COULD FEEL THE ORB BREATHING NEW ENERGY INTO MY BODY..."
"IT WAS ABSORBING EVERYTHING AROUND ME."
"IT WAS HUNGRY."
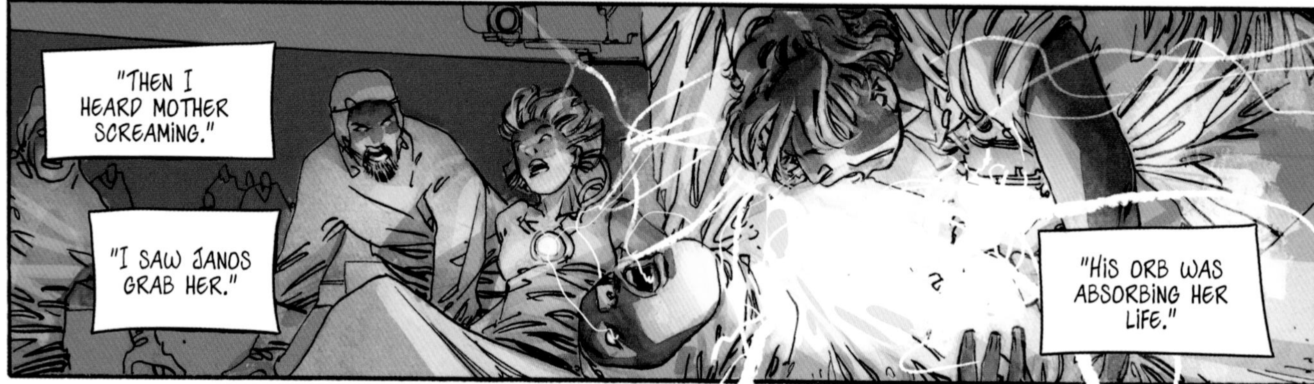
"THEN I HEARD MOTHER SCREAMING."
"I SAW JANOS GRAB HER."
"HIS ORB WAS ABSORBING HER LIFE."

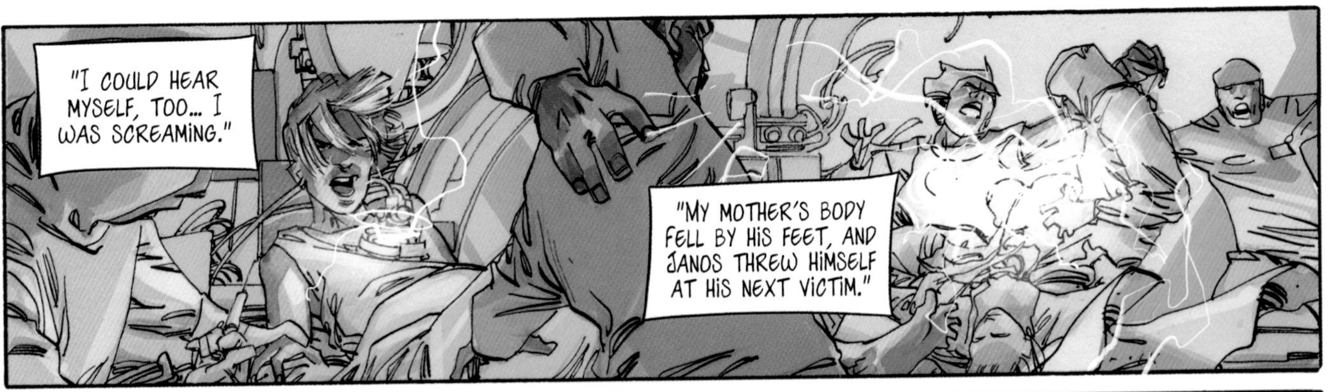
"I COULD HEAR MYSELF, TOO... I WAS SCREAMING."
"MY MOTHER'S BODY FELL BY HIS FEET, AND JANOS THREW HIMSELF AT HIS NEXT VICTIM."

"SUDDENLY, SHE STOOD UP...
...THE LIGHT OF AN ORB INSIDE HER CHEST."

"SHE HUNGERED..."

"THERE WAS NO LOVE LEFT."

"THE SCREAMING AMPLIFIED. THE NIGHTMARE HAD BEGUN."
"MY ORB WAS ALL THAT I COULD FEEL... ITS HUNGER..."
"...IT WAS STRONGER THAN I WAS."

THEY DRAINED EVERY SOURCE OF ENERGY INSIDE EDEN... IT WAS A DEAD ZONE FOR ALL THOSE WHO COULD NO LONGER DIE...

I THINK I PREFERRED IT WHEN YOU TALKED LESS.

IDIOT.

!

SOLAL!

YOU CAN LET GO OF MY ARM, NOW.

OW...! I DIDN'T MEAN TO...
...SORRY.

WHY? YOU'RE RIGHT TO BE SCARED OF ME.

MOVE!

SHIT!
CROK

SHIT!
CRAK
THUD

I'M NOT SCARED. YOU'RE NOT LIKE THEM.

OH YEAH?
WELL I'M NOT LIKE YOU, EITHER!

YES YOU ARE. YOU CAME TO GET ME. YOU FOUND THE MEDICINE.
YOU'RE FREE TO CHOOSE WHO YOU ARE.

CHOOSE? WITH A BATTERY STUCK INSIDE MY TORSO? AREN'T YOU AFRAID THAT I'LL SUCK UP ALL YOUR LIFE FORCE, WISE GUY?
NO.

COOL, WELL THAT MAKES ONE OF US.

TRY NOT TO SHIT YOURSELVES, B.A.S.T.A.R.D.S.
TK
SHIT.
TCHOK

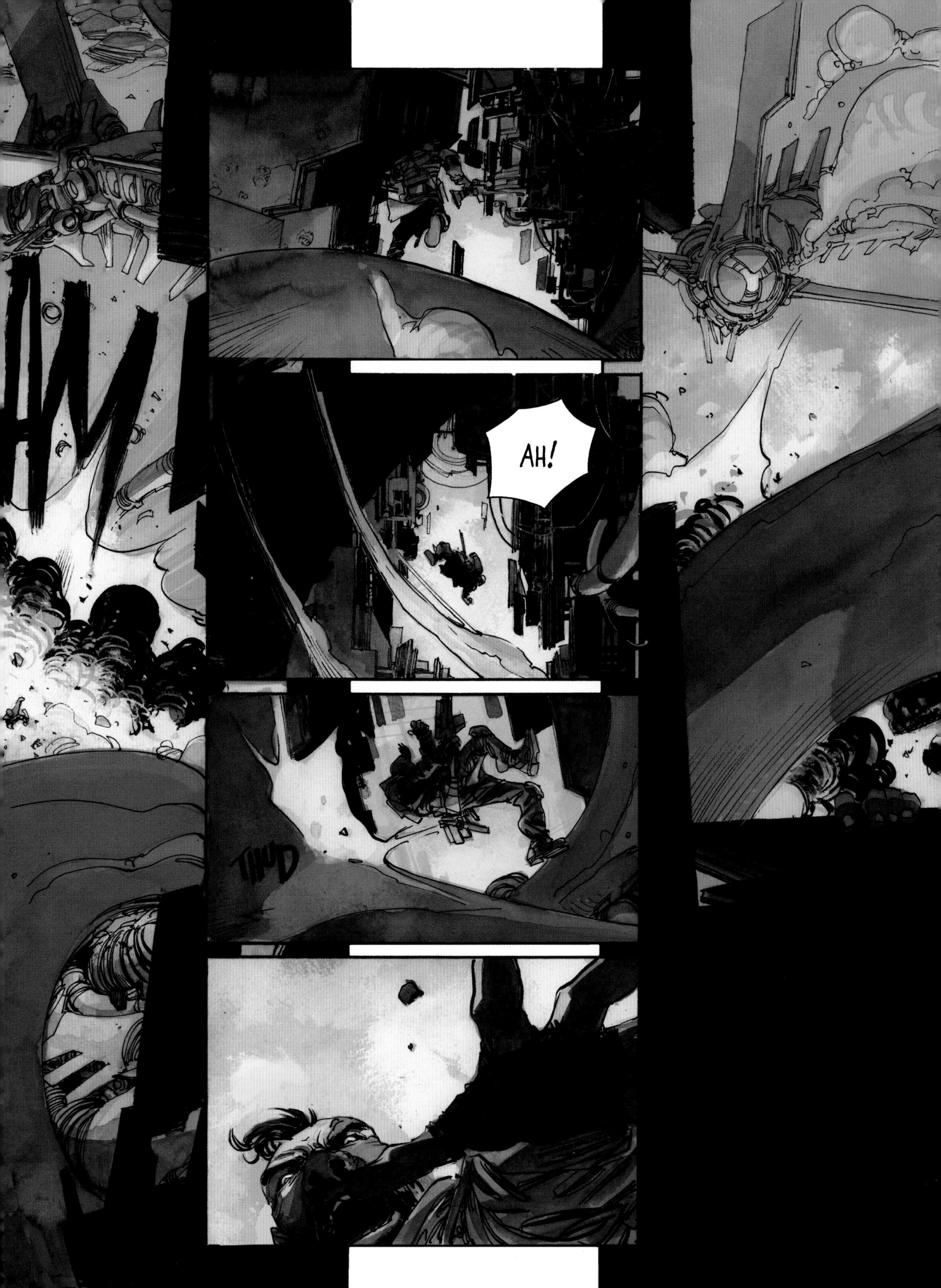
AH!
THUD

WHAT NOW?
JANOS.
"HE KNEW WE'D HAVE TO GO THROUGH THIS DOOR..."
"HE ALWAYS HAS A PLAN..."
"...HE WAS ALWAYS SMARTER THAN ME..."

"HE'S FEEDING OFF HIS TROOPS..."
GOOD THING I WAS ALWAYS DAD'S FAVORITE...
BOOOOOSSHH
OUR SHUTTLE'S HERE!!!
OOOOSSHHH
YOU SAID THEY COULDN'T MOVE!
THEY'RE RUNNING!
RUN FASTER!
GRAB MY ARM!

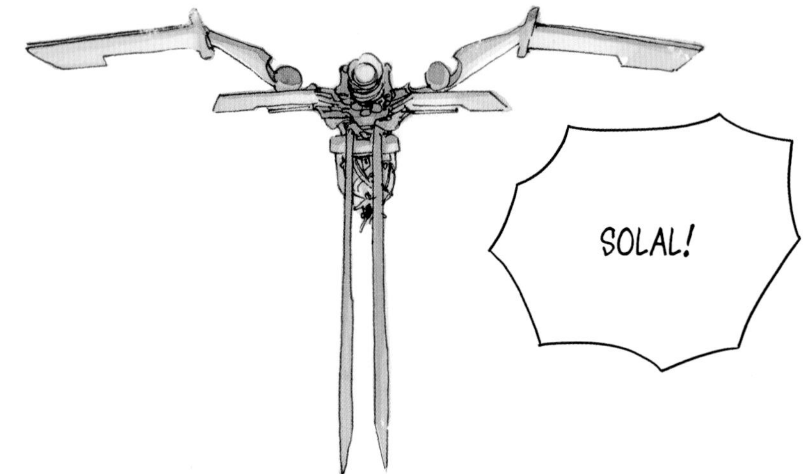
SOLAL!

JEN..
...WE STABILIZED YOUR OB.
YOU HAVE TO REST NOW.

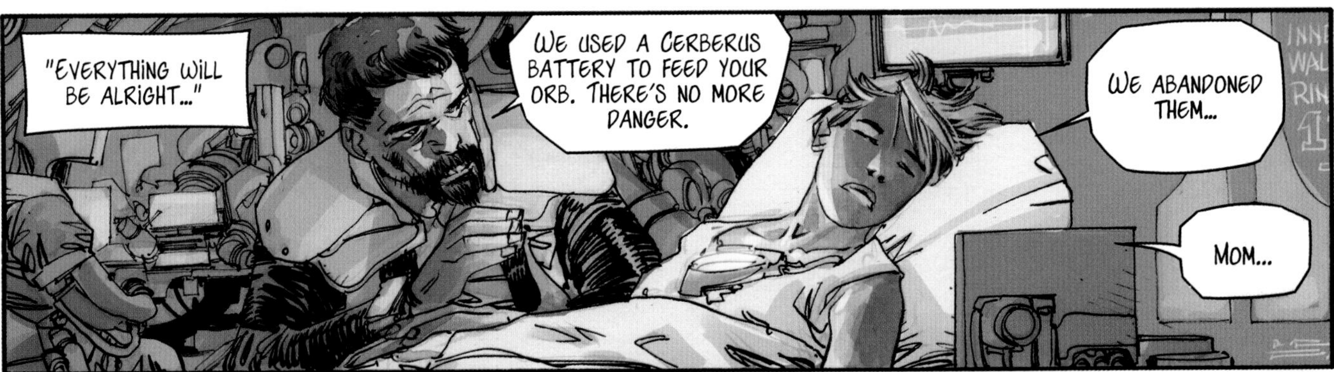
"EVERYTHING WILL BE ALRIGHT..."
WE USED A CERBERUS BATTERY TO FEED YOUR ORB. THERE'S NO MORE DANGER.
WE ABANDONED THEM...
MOM...

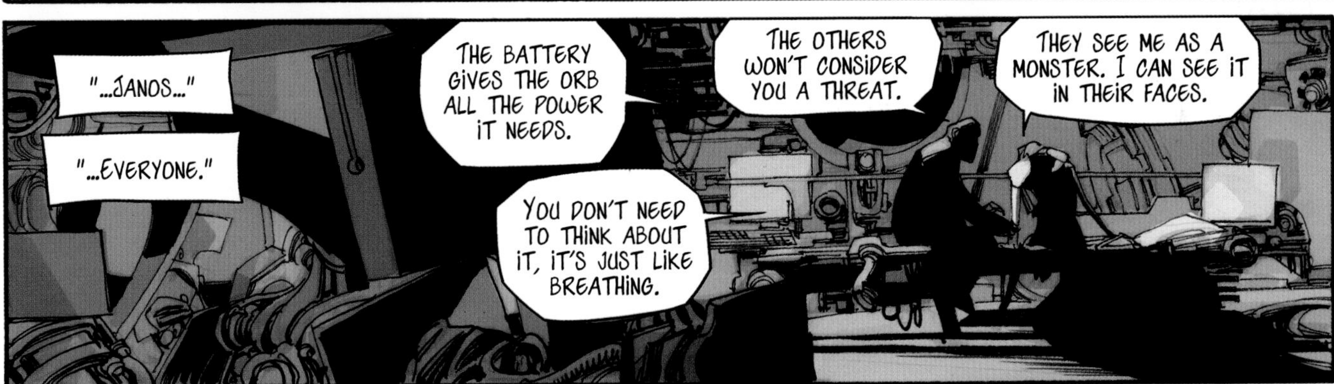
"...JANOS..."
"...EVERYONE."
THE BATTERY GIVES THE ORB ALL THE POWER IT NEEDS.
THE OTHERS WON'T CONSIDER YOU A THREAT.
THEY SEE ME AS A MONSTER. I CAN SEE IT IN THEIR FACES.
YOU DON'T NEED TO THINK ABOUT IT, IT'S JUST LIKE BREATHING.

"I'LL GO LIVE WITH THE CYBERLINGS. ALONE."
I'LL PILOT THE DRONES. I'LL BE CERBERUS'S AIMING SYSTEM.
IT'S YOUR CHOICE.
MY CHOICE?! I WAS BORN IN THIS BOX...

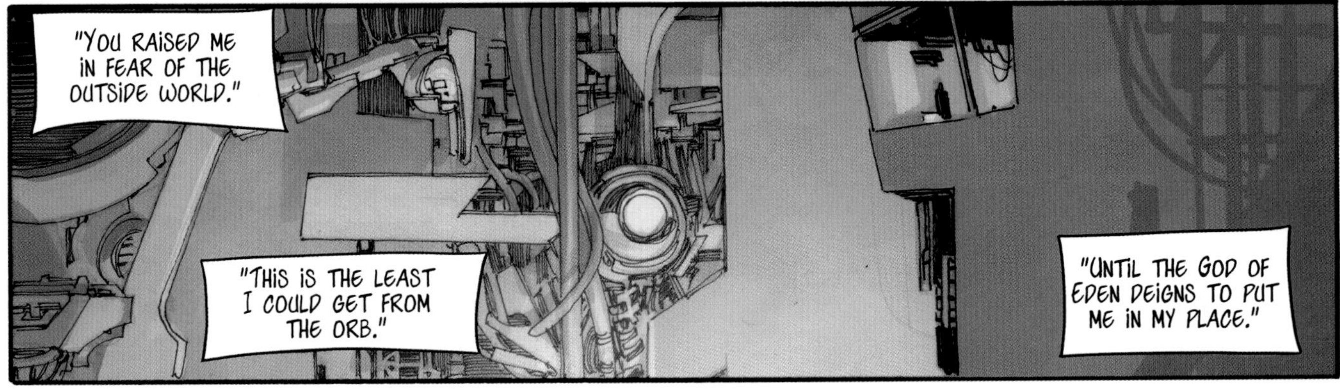
"YOU RAISED ME IN FEAR OF THE OUTSIDE WORLD."
"THIS IS THE LEAST I COULD GET FROM THE ORB."
"UNTIL THE GOD OF EDEN DEIGNS TO PUT ME IN MY PLACE."

"NEITHER LIVING NOR DEAD... THE CAT REVEALS HIMSELF."
GRAB HOLD OF THIS!
EVA!
YOU REALLY ARE A LITTLE TIGRESS!

SCAN
COMPLETE!
EXIT
AUTHORIZED.

THEY OPENED THE DOOR!
THE UNDEAD ARE INSIDE! THEY'RE COMING!
WE HAVE TO CONTAIN THEM!
STOP THEM AT ALL COSTS!
RAHHH
WE CAN'T LET THEM REACH THE EXTERIOR WALLS!

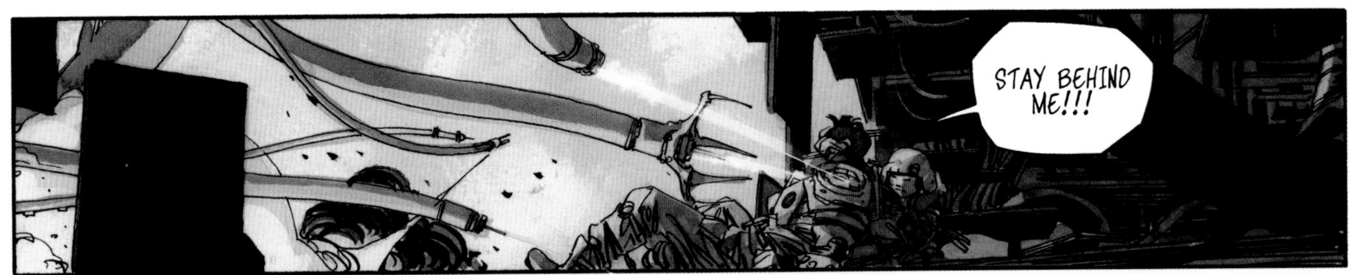
STAY BEHIND ME!!!

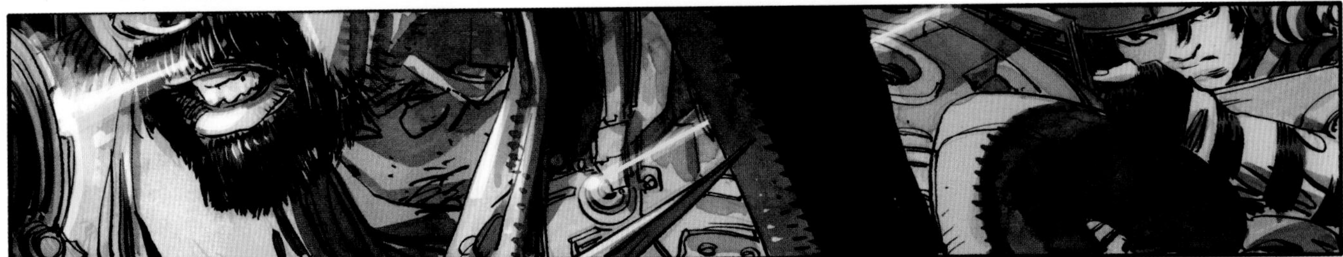

THEY'RE FALLING BACK...
HEY!
THIS IS FOR KARL, B.A.S.T.A.R.D.!
NOMEN OMEN.
BANG

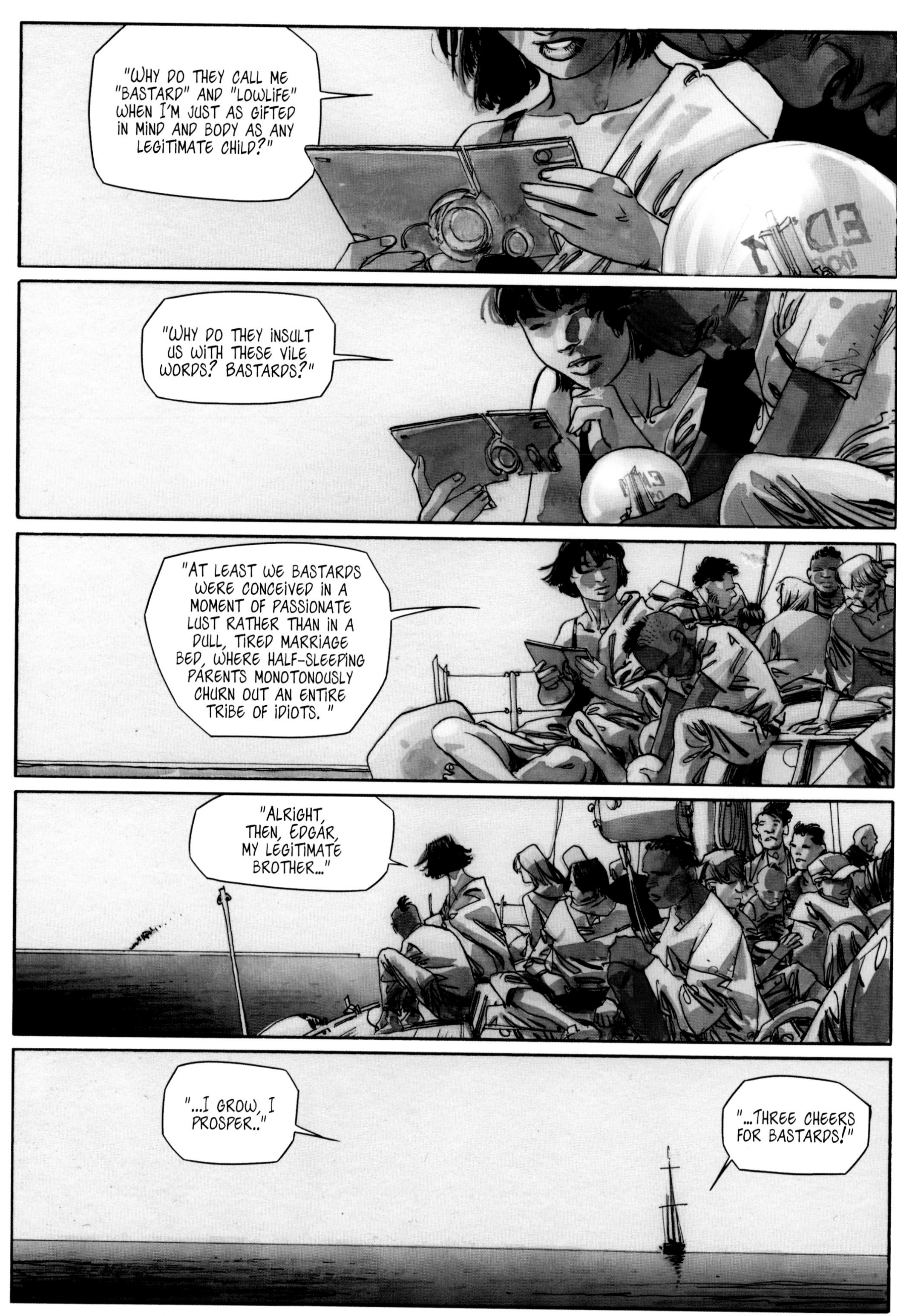
"WHY DO THEY CALL ME "BASTARD" AND "LOWLIFE" WHEN I'M JUST AS GIFTED IN MIND AND BODY AS ANY LEGITIMATE CHILD?"
"WHY DO THEY INSULT US WITH THESE VILE WORDS? BASTARDS?"
"AT LEAST WE BASTARDS WERE CONCEIVED IN A MOMENT OF PASSIONATE LUST RATHER THAN IN A DULL, TIRED MARRIAGE BED, WHERE HALF-SLEEPING PARENTS MONOTONOUSLY CHURN OUT AN ENTIRE TRIBE OF IDIOTS."
"ALRIGHT, THEN, EDGAR, MY LEGITIMATE BROTHER..."
"...I GROW, I PROSPER.."
"...THREE CHEERS FOR BASTARDS!"

CHAPTER 3 – HOMO HOMINI SPES

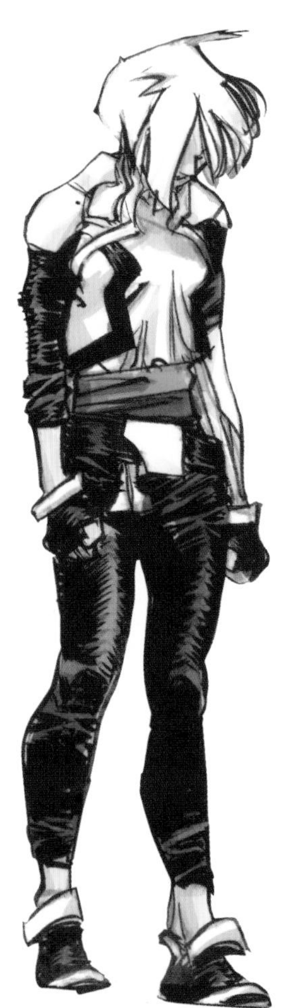

HANF
HANF
HANF
HANF
HANF
TIGRESS!
HAN
HAN
HAN

Armed intervention group is ready for action.

Avoid any direct engagement! Just slow them down!

Reroute all energy away from the undead's path.
We need to deprive them of any source of nourishment.

And how do you plan on doing that, Noah? The transformers draw them in like moths to a flame.

What do you propose, Cliff? That we cut the power supply from the dam?
Exactly, Noah. This place is a tomb.
Let the darkness have it.

Intruders detected!

Close the wall and handle the intruders.

Where's the drone?

The drone isn't responding, sir.

Drone? Please respond.

SOLAL.

YOU'RE ALIVE!
I'M COLD...

HE ABSORBED ALMOST ALL YOUR BODY HEAT AND SPIT YOU RIGHT BACK OUT...
I CAN'T... MOVE...
YOU'RE NOTHING MORE THAN A HUSK TO THEIR ORBS...

...BUT MY BATTERY IS ANOTHER STORY...
...AND THEY'VE SENSED IT.

THE... THE MEDICINE...
IN YOUR POCKET!

It's... It's my fault... All of this.
Shut up.

Shit.

You can't have him!

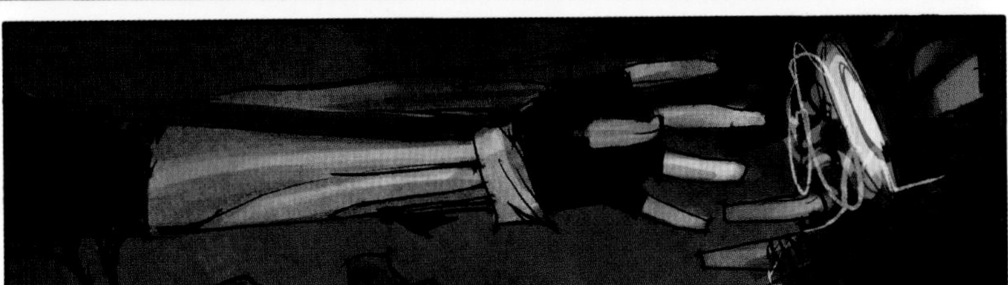

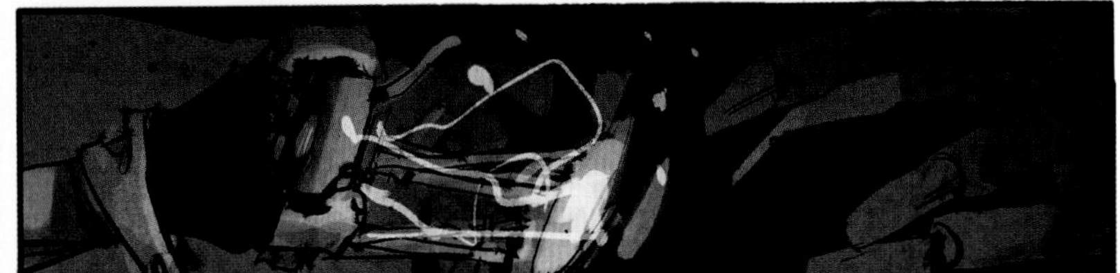

Drone. Please respond!
Come on, Solal! Get up!
Jen!

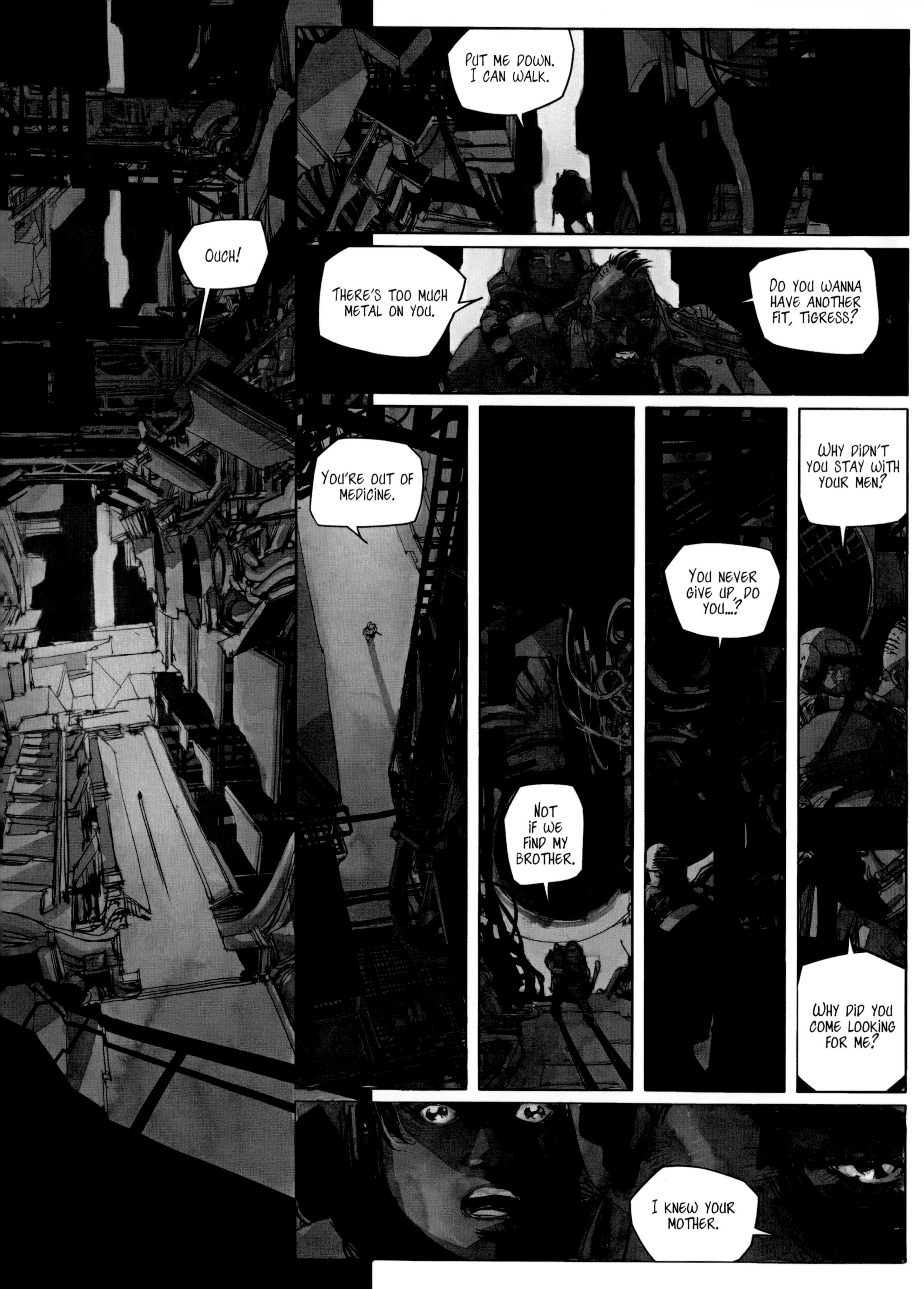
PUT ME DOWN. I CAN WALK.
OUCH!
THERE'S TOO MUCH METAL ON YOU.
DO YOU WANNA HAVE ANOTHER FIT, TIGRESS?
YOU'RE OUT OF MEDICINE.
NOT IF WE FIND MY BROTHER.
YOU NEVER GIVE UP, DO YOU...?
WHY DIDN'T YOU STAY WITH YOUR MEN?
WHY DID YOU COME LOOKING FOR ME?
I KNEW YOUR MOTHER.

"SHE SAVED MY LIFE WHEN I WAS ABOUT YOUR AGE..."

"...SHE FOUND ME SHELTER WHEN I THOUGHT EVERYTHING WAS HOPELESS."

"ME AND MANY OTHERS."

"I CAN SAY IT NOW: YOU HAVE THE SAME LOOK SHE USED TO HAVE..."
"...WHEN SHE DISAPPROVED OF WHAT I WAS DOING."

"YOUR MOM WAS ONE OF THE PEOPLE WHO CREATED EDEN. SHE WOULD READ US STORIES FROM HER CONSOLE..."
"...IN THE HOPES THAT WE'D LEARN TO FORGIVE..."

I'VE ALWAYS BELIEVED THAT...

...HER CONSOLE WAS OUR KEY TO EDEN.

AIM FOR THE ORBS!

POW

THE ORBS!

POW

POW POW

WHERE'S THAT DOOR THAT YOUR BROTHER OPENED?
CAN'T YOU ASK YOUR CONSOLE?
WHY DON'T WE JUST ASK THEM?
CRAP, WHERE DID THEY ALL GO?!
INTRUDERS!
PUT DOWN YOUR WEAPONS AND FOLLOW US TO THE SAFE ZONE!
SHOW THEM THE CONSOLE! NOW!
THIS TERMINAL IS REGISTERED TO LAURA CHO.
WHERE IS SHE?

"SHIT."
I'VE NEVER FOUGHT LIKE THIS! IT DOESN'T STOP!
STAY BEHIND COVER! DON'T MAKE IT ANY EASIER FOR THAT THING!

Maybe it'll stop if it doesn't find a target...
..But it never seems to stop looking... We can't even compete. It's not fair!
Look!
Hey, Marcelo! I don't like it when you let the food get cold!
Shit!
Run! Take shelter!

Sir... The undead have broken past our first line of defense... They're heading for the transformer...
WARNING
WARNING
WARNING
WARNING
Noah... You need to recognize that you can't stop the inevitable. Think about the outside world.
You're in that much of a hurry to die, Cliff?
Solal!
...so...
...cold...
Live.
Please...

SPRAKKKK
WHAT WAS THAT?!
THE SITE HAS BEEN COMPROMISED.
HEAD FOR THE SAFE ZONE.

VOLTAGE DROP AT THE MAIN TRANSFORMER STATION.
SYSTEM INTEGRITY CORRUPTED.
NOAH! I BEG YOU!
THIS HAS GONE TOO FAR!

SHUT UP, CLIFFORD!
I KNOW WHAT I'M DOING!
THE SENSORS HAVE PICKED UP THE DRONE IN ITS DOCK, SIR.

FINALLY!

LOCK THAT YOUNG MAN UP.
GUARDS!
JEN, WE HAVE SOME URGENT PRIORITIES...

STAY DOWN, YOU LITTLE SHIT.
...AND YOU'RE NOT GOING TO LIKE THEM.
DAD, WAIT!

SOMETHING INCREDIBLE HAPPENED.
MY ORB LET OUT HEAT! IT SAVED HIM!

I CAN CONTROL THE ORB!
IT WORKS!
JUST LIKE YOU SAID IT WOULD.

OF COURSE IT WORKS.

BUT TRY TO DO IT WITHOUT A CERBERUS BATTERY INSIDE YOU...
...YOU WOULDN'T BE ABLE TO CONTROL THE ORB WITHOUT A CONTINUAL SOURCE OF ENERGY.

GIVING IS A LUXURY THAT ONLY THOSE WITH ENOUGH TO SPARE CAN ENJOY.

THE OTHERS WILL ALWAYS TAKE WHILE ASKING FOR MORE AND MORE.

WHETHER WE'RE TALKING ABOUT THE PEOPLE ON THE OTHER SIDE OF THE WALL...
...OR THE UNDEAD AND THEIR ORBS...
..."MORE" IS THE ONLY WORD THEY UNDERSTAND.
YOU'RE WRONG.

I CAN HELP YOU, SIR. LET ME FIND MY SISTER...

...B.A.S.T.A.R.D. IS GOING TO LAUNCH ANOTHER ATTACK!
NO NEED TO WORRY...

...CERBERUS IS MAKING SURE THEY'LL NEVER THREATEN US AGAIN.
WHAT?!
NO!

LET GO OF ME!
TO THE DRONE! NOW!

GET A HOLD OF YOURSELF!

SOLAL!

LET GO OF ME!

COUGH
HANF HANF
EVA...?
EVA!
SHE'S HAVING A HARD TIME BREATHING...
WHERE'S HER MEDICINE?
B.A.S.T.A.R.D.!
HOLD ON, EVA!
HERE...
I KNEW IT... KOF!
...I KNEW YOU WEREN'T DEAD.

DEPLOY CERBERUS.
YOU.
RAHH!
BANG
BANG
SOLAL...

RUN!

JEN!
YOU SON OF A BITCH...

I'M GOING TO KILL YOU!

NO!
SOLAL!
CYBERLINGS!
DEPLOY!

DAD!
NO!

LET GO OF ME!

BANG

RATIONS
BANG
BANG

LET ME HELP THEM!
BANG

FORGIVE ME, JEN.
CLAK
NO!
THUD!

YOU LEFT ME NO CHOICE.

YOU WON'T GET AWAY THIS TIME!

JEN!

JEN!
CLIK
CLIK
CLIK
CLIK
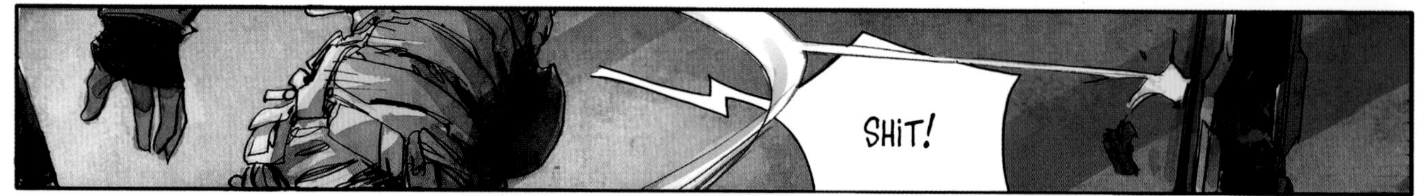
SHIT!

B.A.S.T.A.R.D!
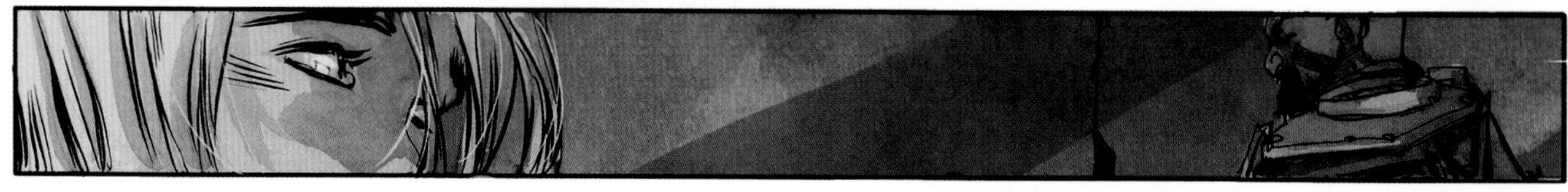

HIDE...
AND THEN JUMP.

SHIT!
WHAT NOW?
SHE SAID JUMP!

CLIFF!

I HAVE THE BATTERY!

BRING THEM ALL BACK INSIDE!

CLIFFORD!

HSSS

NO!
HSSS

THUD

JANOS.

HERE.
TAKE IT.

IT SHOULD'VE BEEN YOURS ALREADY.
BUT KNOW THAT I ALWAYS ACTED IN YOUR BEST INTERESTS.

YOUR PLACE IS IN EDEN.

GO BACK.

JANOS.

NO!

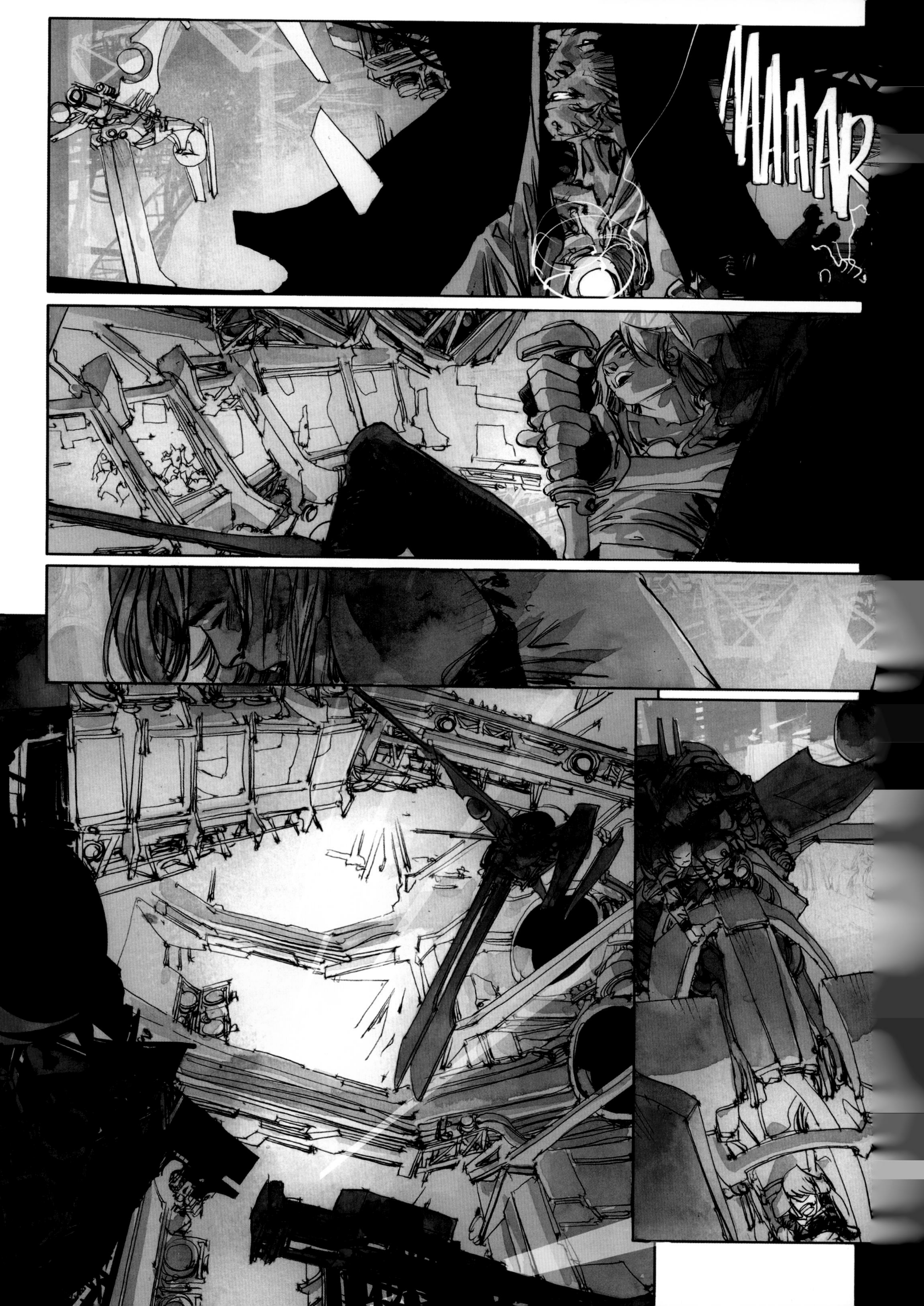
MAAAR

WHAT THE HELL IS GOING ON HERE?
JEN?
THIS WAS SUPPOSED TO BE PARADISE BUT IT'S FULL OF DEMONS...
UGH!
HE TOOK IT, SOLAL.
MY DAD...
...HE TOOK MY BATTERY.
AND NOW JANOS HAS IT. I WON'T BE ABLE TO RESIST THE ORB'S HUNGER... I'M GOING TO TRANSFORM.
NO YOU WON'T.
SOLAL... THE DRONE IS SUSTAINING ME NOW AND I CAN BARELY CONTROL MYSELF.
IT'S JUST A MATTER OF TIME.
YOU CAN RESIST, JEN. WE CAN DO IT.

I KNOW WHAT YOU'RE THINKING.
YOU'RE NOT LIKE THEM.

BUT, I AM... THAT'S HOW I WAS ABLE TO SNEAK PAST THEM TO SAVE YOUR CUTE LITTLE BUTT...

...AGAIN.

YOU.

I DON'T CARE WHO SAVED YOU OR HOW MANY FUCKING TIMES...
BASTARD, WAIT! SHE'S ON OUR SIDE! LET ME EXPLAIN!

SHE HAS A THING IN HER CHEST.
JUST LIKE THOSE DEMONS. IF SHE THINKS SHE'S GONNA TRANSFORM...
...I SAY WE SLIT HER THROAT. SHE'S THE DRONE PILOT, DAMN IT!

BUT SHE JUST SAVED OUR LIVES! PLEASE...
WAIT!

EVERYBODY CALM DOWN. SOLAL, B.A.S.T.A.R.D. KNEW MOM... SHE SAVED HIM WHEN HE WAS LITTLE...
SHE WAS ALSO FROM EDEN.
YOUR MOM?

THAT'S WHY THE DOOR OPENED FOR YOU.

DOESN'T MATTER...
...WE HAVE TO SEAL THIS PLACE AND LOCK THE UNDEAD INSIDE...
...AND STOP CERBERUS FROM MASSACRING THOSE PEOPLE OUTSIDE...
WE'RE THE ONLY ONES WHO CAN DO IT...

...And I'll be dead in less than an hour.
Jen.
You said the battery came from a Cerberus?

There's another one outside. Take off, stop the Cerberus, and take its battery.

Or maybe I take the drone and use Cerberus to get rid of all those creatures and their damn lamps...
No.

No? That damn robot has enough blood on its hull. It's time for Edeners to get their due!

There are no more Edeners. Only the undead are left. They'll transform the entire world into monsters if we let them....
Unless we lead them back into Eden.

I'm sorry, Jen. It's the only way.

So in the end you want to use me as bait to lead them back inside.
And here I thought you liked me...

I... that's not what I...
I think he does...
Be quiet, Eva.

You asked me what I would do if it was my family, Jen. I told you that I didn't know. And that's still true.
But we're talking about the people who led the world to ruin now.

Who are getting ready to condemn what little is left.
I say we turn off the sun and let them sleep in the dark.

And how will you do that, grease monkey? Just flick off the switch?
You and I will stay here.
And Jen will tell us what to do.

The transformer station.

THAT WOULD BE MY FATHER'S PLAN. GET THEM ALL TOGETHER IN THE SAME PLACE THEN DRAW THEM INSIDE WITH MY BATTERY...

...THEN HE'D STOP THE TRANSFORMER STATION AFTER LOCKING THEM ALL INSIDE.
THE DEAD CATS BACK INSIDE THEIR BOX.

MY BROTHER HAS MY BATTERY...
...THE DARKNESS WON'T KILL HIM.

HE'LL WANT MORE. YOUR DAD WAS RIGHT ABOUT THAT.
GO TAKE THE CERBERUS BATTERY. PUT AN END TO THE MASSACRE AND SAVE YOURSELF.
YOU HAVE TO GET THERE BEFORE JANOS DOES.
SHE'S THE ONE WHO FOUND YOUR MEDICINE, YOU KNOW...

SO, YOU MET OUR MOTHER WHEN YOU WERE JUST A KID...
GUESS THAT SORT OF MAKES YOU OUR BIG BROTHER...?

DON'T PUSH YOUR LUCK, KID.

B.A.S.T.A.R.D... THAT'S WHAT THEY CALL YOU NOW?

WE'RE ALL BASTARDS HERE.

THE CHILDREN, TOO?

AS LONG AS THAT WALL STILL STANDS...
...WE'LL NEVER FORGET.
AND WE'LL NEVER FORGIVE.

SHE LEFT TWO DAYS LATER...
WE SHOULD BLOW THEM ALL UP.
AND THEN WHAT?
TAKE THEIR PLACE?
KEEP EDEN FOR OURSELVES?
BECAUSE THAT'S WHAT THEY DID...
...THEY HOARDED THE FUTURE AND DAMNED THEMSELVES!

"I WANT TO
BELIEVE WE
CAN DO BETTER
THAN THAT..."

IT STOPPED!

THE WALL'S OPENING!

SOMETHING'S COMING OUT.

WAIT... THERE'S SOMETHING ELSE...

B.A.S.T.A.R.D.!
"SOLAL!"
"THE RADIO FREQUENCY IS OPEN."
NOMEN OMEN!
WAIT.
B.A.S.T.A.R.D.?!
FIRE ON EVERYTHING THAT'S COMING OUT OF THE WALL!
THAT'S A FUCKING ORDER!

WELL...

...IF IT'S AN ORDER...

WE SHOOT FIRST...
POW
...ASK QUESTIONS LATER.
JEN!
WE'RE IN THE TRANSFORMER CONTROL ROOM!

THE UNDEAD ARE BUSY ABSORBING ENERGY AND HAVEN'T DETECTED US YET... BUT THAT'LL CHANGE AS SOON AS I TURN THIS OFF.
DID YOU GET THE BATTERY?

NO, THE... THE DRONE IS FAILING...

"SOLAL, DO YOU READ ME?"

"I ABSORBED THE DRONE'S ENERGY..."

IT'S GONNA CRASH...

END TRANSMISSION.

WHAT ARE THEY DOING?

"...CLIMBING ONTO CERBERUS!"
THEY WANT THE MONSTER!
SOLAL! I'M BACK!
I'LL BRING YOU CERBERUS.
BANG
BANG
JEN! WE'RE UNDER ATTACK HERE!
BANG
TURN THAT SHIT OFF! THEY'RE ON US!
JEN! THEY'RE LOOKING FOR SOMETHING AROUND HERE! AND IT'S NOT THE STATION!
SO... SOLAL...
MOM'S CONSOLE IS ON...
CHARGE COMPLETED

WELCOME TO ED3N
"WELCOME TO EDEN"? SERIOUSLY?
ALL OF YOU GO FUCK YOURSELVES!
TAKE EVA AND GET OUT OF HERE!
NOW, DAMN IT!
RRAAAAHHHH!
POW
"SOLAL!"
"I'M INSIDE!"
"SOLAL! CAN YOU HEAR ME?"
THE UNDEAD ARE ABSORBING CERBERUS! IT'S BREAKING DOWN!
I HAVE TO GET OUT OF HERE!
JEN, END TRANSMISSION!

LET GO OF THE CONSOLE! THAT'S WHAT THEY WANT!
HANF HANF
KOF! KOF!
HOLD ON!
WE CAN MAKE IT!
SOLAL!
KOF!
LOOK!

JANOS.

WE CAN STILL...
WE CAN STILL PILOT THE DRONE TOGETHER. PLEASE...

...COME WITH ME--
SWAK

THERE!
THE WALL!
WE CAN MAKE IT!

THE DRONE!

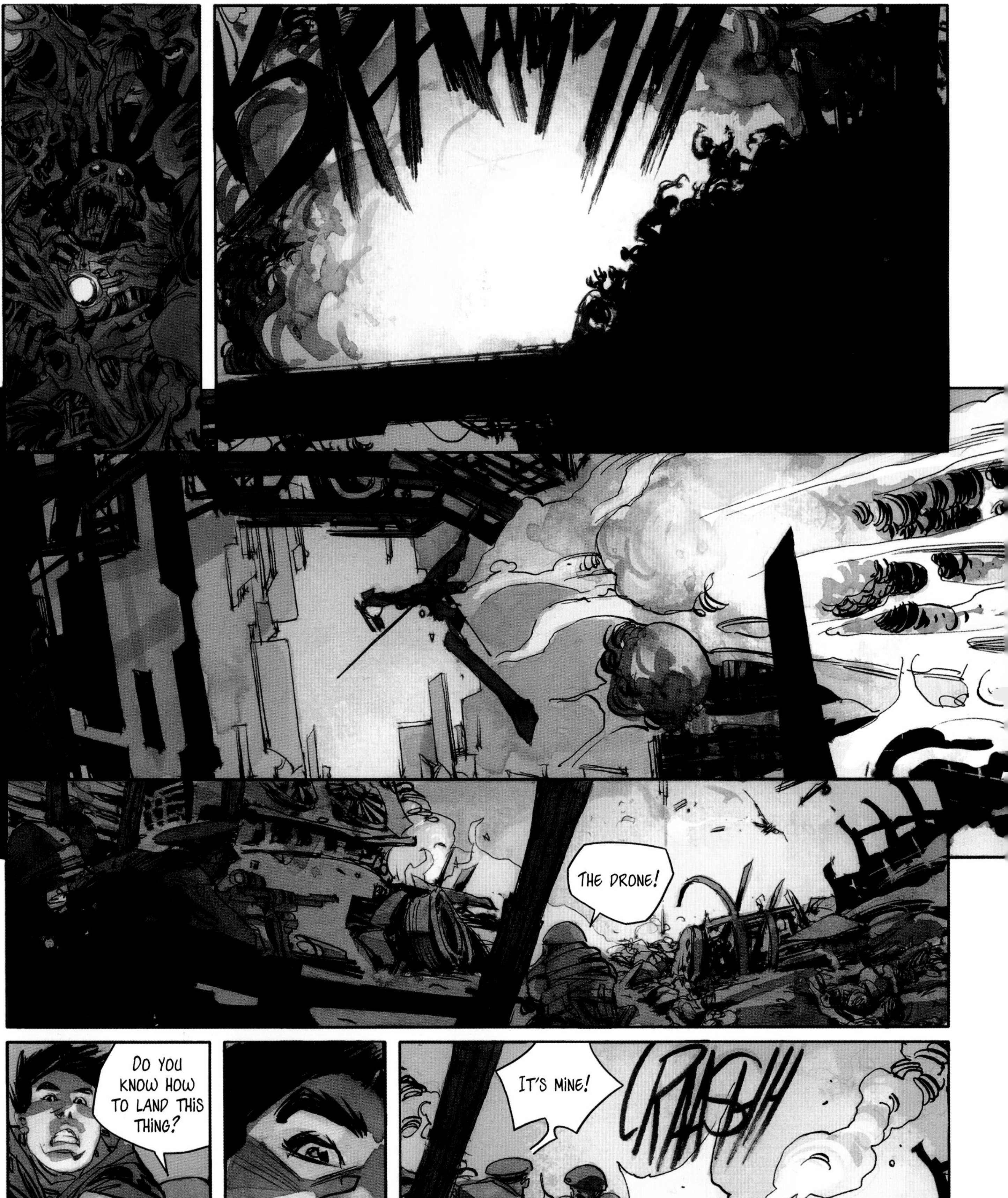

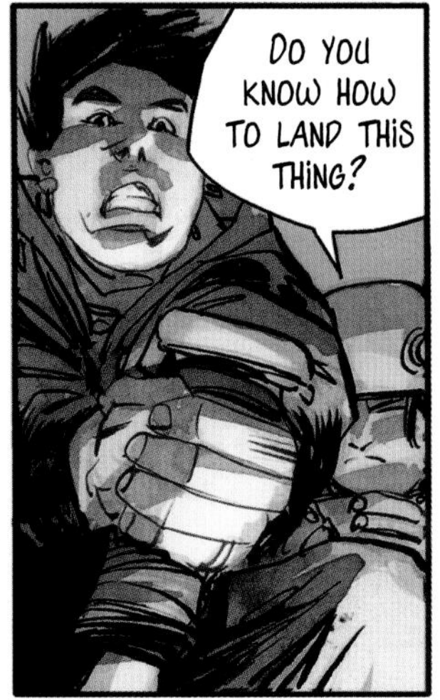
DO YOU KNOW HOW TO LAND THIS THING?

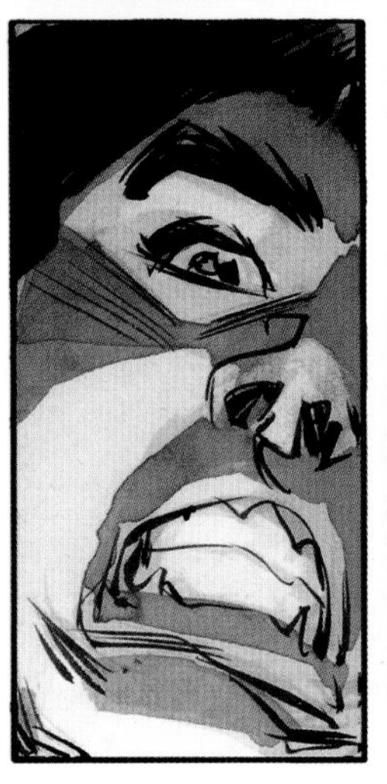

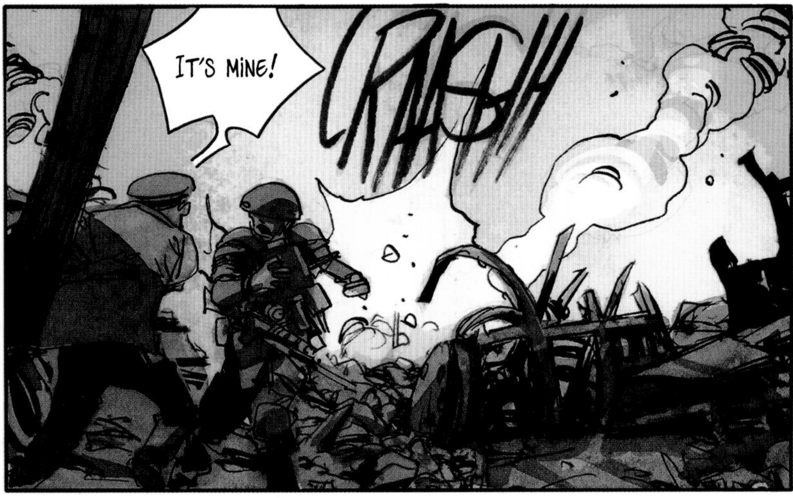
IT'S MINE!

EVA!
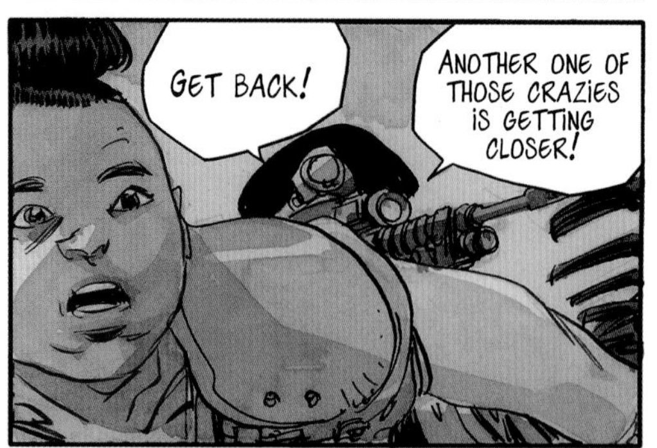
GET BACK!
ANOTHER ONE OF THOSE CRAZIES IS GETTING CLOSER!

DON'T SHOOT!

SHE'S WITH US!
JEN, ARE YOU OKAY?

JEN...?

HSSS
JEN!
RESIST IT!
I...
RE... RES...
JEN!
RESIST!
...RE... SIST...
YOU CAN DO IT!
YOU CAN...

VRR

THERE...

SO... SOLAL...

IS IT WORKING?

WHAT'LL HAPPEN WHEN WE RUN OUT OF POWER?

WILL SHE EAT SOMEONE?

VRR

NO.
SHE'S STRONGER THAN THE ORB...

...AND THE BATTERY FROM MOM'S CONSOLE CAN FEED HER.

OKAY, JEN. YOU CAN KEEP THE BATTERY.
EVEN IF SOLAL ALWAYS CALLED IT A DUMB THING.
HE NEVER UNDERSTOOD...

...THE REASON I NEVER TURNED IT ON WAS BECAUSE I WAS TOO AFRAID OF LOSING ALL THE STORIES MOM TOLD US.
BUT I KNOW THEM BY HEART NOW!

WILL... WILL YOU SHARE THEM WITH ME?
I'D LIKE THAT.

YOU DON'T KNOW WHAT YOU'RE ASKING FOR...
JERK.

CHANDRA
KARL
THE WALL HAD
WHY DID CHANDRA DO THAT? IT WAS POINTLESS.
WE'RE NOT ALL FREE TO CHOOSE, MY BOY.
B.A.S.T.A.R.D. WAS.
WHAT WOULD HE SAY?

SHIT.

JEN!

THE NEW BATTERY IS LESS POWERFUL... IT MIGHT HAVE BEEN A PROTOTYPE...
YOU'LL HAVE TO RECHARGE IT.
I BUILT YOU THIS.
IT WORKS OFF SOLAR ENERGY.

WHAT?
NOTHING.
I'M NOT AFRAID OF YOU.

REMEMBER ME?

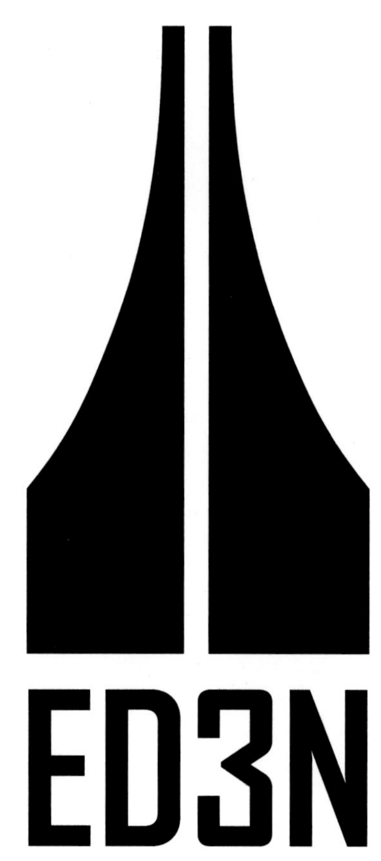
ED3N

MARIO ALBERTI 2017
B.A.S.T.A.R.D.
project
ED3N

10%
THE COMMANDER
project
ED3N
ED3N
CLOSED
ED3N
MARIO ALBERTI 2017

project
ED3N
ASGJ 33442-5653
5678-DFSGFDF-1
CERBERUS
56456
- 6767
CVCX
project
ED3N
MARIO ALBERTI 2017

JEN
project
ED3N

project
ED3N

SOLAL & EVE
project
ED3N
MARIO ALBERTI 2017

The Authors

Mario Alberti

He's been drawing comic books since he was old enough to hold a pencil and plans to continue until he is no longer able to do so...

"Antoine" by Charreyron

As far back as I can remember, I have always had a pencil in my hand. I drew all the time and everywhere. But unlike others, it was always little stories, more storyboards than detailed drawings. As a comic book fan, my first literary emotions were for the likes of *The New Mutants* and *Akira* which took root in my head with the first issue casually purchased in a small neighborhood bookstore.

My passion for original worlds and heroic stories naturally found its place when I started my career as a director for video game cinematic sequences. *Tomb Raider, 50 Cent: Bulletproof, Godzilla, Dungeons & Dragons, Terminator 3...* My early years literally immersed me in epic battles and excess. In the process, I created my first animated series: *Galactik Football,* a space soccer series where matches were filmed like action scenes.

Always in search of original worlds, I joined Mathieu Kassovitz's live action film *Babylon A.D.* starring Vin Diesel. In 2011, my first feature film as Director, *The Prodigies,* was released, an animated adaptation of the novel *La Nuit des Enfants Rois* by Bernard Lenteric. Its screening in Cannes will remain an incredible moment for me. As a kid, I never thought I'd one day be part of this kind of adventure.

My dreams continued when I had the good fortune of crossing paths with Christophe Arleston to direct the *Lanfeust Quest* series, the animated adaptation of one of my favorite French comic series since high school: *Lanfeust de Troy.*

After finishing with Hébus, I set foot in the video game industry again working on *Detroit: Become Human.* But a new era began in 2017 when I left the animation world for "live action," directing episodes of the suspense series *Transferts* for Arte. Awarded at the 2017 Séries Mania international Festival, this was the opportunity for me to start a new adventure in a world where, more than anywhere else, the characters and the story are at the center of everything.

By the time you read this, I'll most likely be creating an e-sports project or exploring virtual Paris in a movie called *Neo Paris.* Original universes have always fascinated me and, before my career is over, I hope to adapt *The Wall* to the screen and bring the adventures of Solal and Eva to life.

ED3N